# WEDDING
# PLANNING
## *Unmasked!*

*Revealing the knowledge that experienced wedding professionals*

*consider essential for couples planning a wedding*

## JANIS FLAGG

ISBN (print book):  978-1-7321646-9-7
Available in eBook format

Cover design by Kathryn E. Campbell

Printed by Gorham Printing in the United States of America

*Legacy* ONE AUTHORS
Kirkland, WA

LegacyOneAuthors.com

# CONTENTS

# ACKNOWLEDGMENTS

Thank you to the wedding vendors who have contributed wisdom and experience for this book. I am honored to work with you, to learn from you, and to share the deepest level of dedication to helping couples fulfill their dreams on their wedding day. Your profession is stressful, yet you are laser focused on best serving your clients. You aren't mind readers, but even when given limited information, you turn on a dime to pull everything together in a professional manner. We are a close-knit profession, no different from any other helping professions. We invest with our hearts and souls and often reap lifelong friendships in return.

Thank you to everyone who in any way, shape, or form helped me navigate the process of writing this book. When I had only one section left to write, a second-opinion doctor confirmed what I suspected during the previous months—that I had a fractured right pinky finger. Yes, the return key finger! Thanks to friends and family for putting up with my occasional loud "ows" and grimacing face. You helped me laugh the pain away.

Published authors, I have a new respect for you! I will never look at a book the same way again—so many different types of editing to ready a book for print! The book is your baby. You can only read it so many times before you need to let it grow up and get out of the house. Thanks to everyone who treated "my baby" with tender loving care.

# INTRODUCTION

"Congratulations! Let me see your ring!"

"I'm impressed."

"Somebody knows how to choose a ring!"

Tired of hearing these comments? Well, enjoy those congrats while they last, but don't be surprised if some "congratulations" sentiments turn into verbal and non-verbal darts of disapproval of your planning choices along the way. The innuendoes sting. Wedding planning is an exercise in psychology, logistics, art, science, and emotion.

This is not a book of lists, though some useful lists are included. This book's purpose is to help you find your own simple way to create a vision that turns into the reality of your wedding. Your wedding is unique. It is no one else's. No two weddings are alike, so why muddle through lists that don't pertain to *your* wedding? What's missing from most wedding books is how to navigate *within each vendor category*, learn what they each do, and know how to work with them as a winning team from the very beginning. I will help you find, focus, and act on your priorities, not create a generic, cookie-cutter wedding. If you are comfortable outside the box or have difficulty moving within the box, this book is for you!

With a few exceptions, *most vendors* prefer that you hire them about twelve months before the wedding. They don't want to be an afterthought, the last to be hired with whatever money is left in your budget. Yet, not every couple wants to wait twelve months to get married, and not all have access to their full budget twelve months prior.

Instead of lists and charts dictating a time frame, I've addressed the stages chronologically, with ample education on how to reduce your costs and how to best work with vendors. Too many lists can pile on unnecessary expenditures, stress, and obligation.

Making milestone events unique, personalized, or comforting comes so naturally to me that friends and families automatically look to me for the planning. After repeatedly being asked, "Do you plan weddings for a living?" I decided the answer is *yes*. Now, after twelve years in the business, I write this book to clear up the misinformation about weddings from various media and sketchy resources. I have seen wedding vendors misrepresented, and I have seen couples receive unstable information about the real world of weddings that leads to unattainable expectations for their own wedding. In this book *I reveal the unfettered truth* about what wedding vendors want people to know about their specialty in the wedding industry, so they can best serve you. Thus, *Wedding Planning—Unmasked!*

You will gain an understanding of what vendors actually do so that your consultations and relationship with them are relaxed and productive from the beginning. Communication is key, and an extra helping of knowledge will benefit you tremendously. "What's your budget?" is not the best way to start a vendor/client relationship. Equally awkward is opening with, "How much do you charge?" Instead, start with a base of knowledge and learn ways to save money that match your priorities. Make new friends, not awkward experiences.

You will learn how to save time, money, or both. For instance, flowers are more expensive depending upon the time of the year they are in bloom and where they are grown. Research and planning to accommodate the season will save you money and headaches.

You'll learn how to go with the flow when the "unexpected" happens. You'll learn to anticipate problems and prevent them. You'll learn how aiming for perfection can add stress and remove joy from the wedding. You will learn to ask yourself who you really *want* to please or feel that you *have to* please. Will they still love you if something goes wrong? What will matter ten years from now? What is the most important part of your wedding day? Is it a "must do," or is it only a preference? Change your "shoulds" into "preferables." Do your feelings change? That rephrasing can help you declutter your process and be happier in the doing.

Everything comes down to psychology, and oh boy, will you ever get to practice that! I'll arm you with some "come-backs" or some "grin and bear its" to help you get through the barrage of ideas and power plays from relatives or friends who seem to have gone berserk. It's fun to beat them at their own game without creating enemies. Win-win!

Things will go more smoothly when you pay attention to learning styles of yourself and others. The more you can assign tasks with that learning style in mind, the more productive everyone will be. Do you learn by hearing, seeing, touching, smelling, tasting, physical activity, or in silence? Honoring your innate style will make your wedding planning easier, more fun, and less costly.

Not everyone fits the same mold. Clients have told me that if they hadn't hired me, it would have taken forever to get married and they would have argued a lot. I will show you how long engagements can be your budget's worst enemy. Whatever the time frame, I'm here to make your wedding planning easier to manage.

You should be able to look back on this event as one of your favorite times. You don't want to wail, "I just want it all over with!" You may feel that way at times, but there are ways to make it fun and keep your sanity in this wedding planning adventure and add to your wedding fund at the same time (see Ban "W" Days in Planning Stage 4).

This book is written in small sections for quick reference. The intention is to educate you about everyone you might or might not hire in the planning process. I call the chapters "Planning Stages," and I highly recommend that you read every one. You will learn things and find better ways to do what you are already considering.

Enough forecasting, already. Turn the page and get on with your adventure!

# PLANNING STAGE

# 1

## The Foundation

# 1

◇◇◇◇◇◇◇◇◇◇◇◇◇◇◇◇◇◇◇◇◇◇◇◇◇◇◇

# Engagement

Congratulations! You're engaged! Are you excited, scared, feeling paralyzed? It's normal. You've not been here before, so naturally the feelings are new and different. Something would be wrong if you weren't even the slightest bit nervous. It's okay. You'll gradually get used to referring to your other half as your fiancé or fiancée. Enjoy this time on cloud nine!

As soon as you have announced your wedding engagement, people will barrage you with questions and opinions about everything from your wedding date to where you're going on your honeymoon. Let's prepare you for that here and now.

**Your best defense is a united front.** This is true not only on the heels of engagement, but throughout the wedding planning process. You will be miles ahead of everyone else if the two of you have already discussed what you want before others try to create your wedding for themselves.

I present a planning tool for my clients at our first consultation, designed to establish priorities and get a bird's-eye view of the wedding. I call it the "Wedding Visionnaire." This tool helps you describe what makes you tick as individuals and discuss your favorite hobbies, alone and together, to develop the overall feel for your wedding. The Visionnaire addresses what your style is and how that will be reflected in your wedding.

Opposites attract, but couples are usually closer to being on the same page than you would imagine when it comes to a wedding. I'm always impressed with the great ideas for wedding details that come from the groom-to-be. The groom's preferences and touches are important, and grooms are now much more involved in wedding planning than in times past. I've found that I can predict what people want for their wedding with a few basic questions, and surprisingly, almost all couples give similar answers. They want simple and elegant or simple and fun. The word *simple* is usually a code word for "don't make it expensive" or "I don't have a huge budget." That works. Now YOU get to complete your own *Wedding Visionnaire*! Here's how:

Choose which of you is Person A and who is Person B. At the beginning of each section are instructions on how to approach the question. Some questions you will answer separately and then go over your results together; others you will answer together right off the bat.

# WEDDING VISIONNAIRE

*SEPARATELY, answer this question and then compare notes.*

1. What are you most excited about when you envision your wedding and reception?

*SEPARATELY, answer this question and then compare notes.*

2. How would you describe what you see from your mind's eye when you envision your wedding and reception?

*SEPARATELY, answer this question and then compare notes.*

3. Choose any of the following that come to your mind when you envision the atmosphere or feeling at your wedding:

## CEREMONY:

a.  Light and airy

b.  Dark and cozy

c.  Elegant

d.  Casual

e.  Fun

f.  Very solemn

g.  Contemporary

h.  Vintage

i.  Traditional

j.  Funky

k.  Loud

l.  Quiet

m. Reflecting nature (outdoor elements)

n.  Urban

o.  Rustic/country

p.  Serious

q.  Humorous

r.  Being surrounded by as many people as possible

s.  Having just a few of your closer friends and family

t.  Bohemian style

4. Which of the following come to mind when you envision the atmosphere or feeling at your wedding *RECEPTION*:

a. Light and airy

b. Dark and cozy

c. Elegant

d. Casual

e. Fun

f. Very solemn

g. Contemporary

h. Vintage

i. Traditional

j. Funky

k. Loud

l. Quiet

m. Reflecting nature (outdoor elements)

n. Urban

o. Rustic/country

p. Serious

q. Humorous

r. Being surrounded by as many people as possible

s. Having just a few of your closer friends and family

t. Bohemian style

*TOGETHER, answer this question.*

5. Which of the following most closely match "your style":

a. I don't want our wedding to be very different from what I've seen or heard of other weddings.

b. I want our wedding to be different from everyone else's, but not too different.

c. I would like our wedding to be somewhat traditional with just a few touches that are different.

d. I would like to be so creative that people remember our wedding as special and unique!

e. I want our wedding to be simple and standard.

f. I want our wedding to be elegant.

g. I want our wedding to be like a fairy tale.

h. I don't know! I just want a wedding and to get it over with!

i. I want it to be the most amazing day of our lives, no expenses spared!

j. I want it to be the most amazing day of our lives, but not too extravagant!

k. I don't mind having a small budget, because there are only a few things that we really want to do at our wedding.

l. I don't mind having a small budget, because I want to do a lot of the fun stuff myself.

----

*TOGETHER, select any answers that apply to this question.*

----

6. My biggest worries about our wedding are:

a. Interference from family and friends

b. The size of the guest list

c. Unexpected expenses

d. Food and beverage costs

e. Finding the right venue

f. Not being able to afford everything that we want to do

g. Not knowing what to do and when

h. Finding the right dress

i. Choosing colors or a theme

j. That people won't dance

k.  That some people won't be watching their kids and it will take away from having a good time

l.  My friend/relative said they want to do _____ for us and we really prefer that they don't

m. That some guests won't get along with each other

n.  Some people will drink too much alcohol resulting in bad or obnoxious behavior

o. Other _____

*Memories are being created by everyone
on your wedding day.*

*TOGETHER, answer this question.*

7. For our *WEDDING CEREMONY*, we want our *GUESTS* to remember:

   a.  How beautiful it was

   b.  How unique it was

   c.  How sentimental it was

   d.  How much fun we had

   e.  That our culture(s) was/were celebrated

   f.  How our friends or family were active participants in the ceremony

   g.  How our missing loved ones were honored

   h.  How our religious practices were honored

   i.  Other _____

8. For our *RECEPTION*, we want our *GUESTS* to remember:

    a.  How beautiful it was

    b.  How unique it was

    c.  How delicious the food was

    d.  The awesome dancing!

    e.  How sentimental it was

    f.  How much fun they had

    g.  That our culture(s) was/were celebrated

    h.  How our guests were honored

    i.  Other _____

*TOGETHER, answer this question.*

9. For our *WEDDING CEREMONY, WE* want to remember most:

    a.  How beautiful it was

    b.  How unique it was

    c.  How sentimental it was

    d.  How much fun we had

    e.  That our culture(s) or was/were celebrated

    f.  How our religious practices were honored

    g.  How our friends or family were active participants in the ceremony

    h.  How our missing loved ones were honored

    i.  Other _____

10. For our *WEDDING RECEPTION, WE* want to remember most:

    a. How beautiful it was

    b. How unique it was

    c. How delicious the food was

    d. The awesome dancing!

    e. How sentimental it was

    f. How much fun everyone had

    g. That my/our culture(s) was/were celebrated

    h. How our guests were honored

    i. Other _____

## NOTES:

# WEDDING & RECEPTION ELEMENTS

*SEPARATELY, rank each wedding and reception element by its importance to you individually. Then each of you select your top five.*

---

---

---

---

---

---

Next, to combine your lists to come up with the top three or four. These are the areas you will emphasize for your budget.

*SEPARATELY, rank these elements of a wedding and then compare notes.*

11. On a scale of 1-5, with 1 being least important and 5 being most important, rank the following for things you want most for your wedding and reception combined.

Level of Priority: 1 = least. 5 = most.

## Wedding & Reception Elements Priorities

(Alphabetical)

1  2  3  4  5   Alcohol

1  2  3  4  5   Attendant's dresses

1  2  3  4  5   Cake

1  2  3  4  5   Dancing

1  2  3  4  5   Decorations

1  2  3  4  5   DJ

1  2  3  4  5   Entertainment

1  2  3  4  5   Favors

1  2  3  4  5   Flowers for aisle, altar

1  2  3  4  5   Flowers for tables

1  2  3  4  5   Flowers to carry

1  2  3  4  5   Flowers to wear

1  2  3  4  5   Food, beverages

1  2  3  4  5   Hair and makeup

1  2  3  4  5   Honoring those who have passed away

1  2  3  4  5   Invitations and Save-The-Dates

1  2  3  4  5   Musicians/vocalists

1  2  3  4  5   Photo booth

1  2  3  4  5   Photography

1  2  3  4  5   Slide show

1  2  3  4  5   Table decorations

1  2  3  4  5   Transportation (i.e., limo, classic car, horse-drawn carriage, etc.)

1  2  3  4  5   Tuxedos

1  2  3  4  5   Veil

1  2  3  4  5   Venue

1  2  3  4  5   Videography

1  2  3  4  5   Wedding dress*

* The wedding dress is sometimes not included in a budget but as a completely separate item unto itself.

## Wedding & Reception Elements (Continued)

Now that you each know your priorities,
narrow them down to your top 5:

_____

_____

_____

_____

_____

_____

_____

_____

_____

_____

*TOGETHER narrow the list down to 3 or 4. Your top priorities
will determine your focus for your budget. Stay tuned for
a slight twist regarding honeymoons that might help you
increase your budget to add another priority or two!*

# 2

◇◇◇◇◇◇◇◇◇◇◇◇◇◇◇◇◇◇◇◇◇◇◇◇◇◇

# Budget

In the end, you should have a compromise with what you want while considering what accommodates your budget or other people's financial contributions.

**Guest count.** The single biggest factor in the cost of a wedding is the number of guests. Have a ballpark idea of how many guests will attend your wedding. Will you limit your guest list to very close friends and family? This may be your first exposure to unsolicited advice or input. Let's say you want a small wedding with fewer than a hundred people. That can change quickly when your mother insists that her cousin (whom you barely know) would be horrified if not invited to the wedding. There will be people that even you forgot to include whom you definitely want to invite. Small weddings usually turn into larger weddings, but everyone somehow survives.

The guest count affects everything from invitations to food budget and the size of the venue. Everything—tables, linens, chairs, centerpieces to stemware—is affected by the guest count. RSVPs dictate the cake size (and leftover cake). The issue of RSVPs can get messy. When people don't send in their RSVPs and expect to be fed, it's a problem. Likewise, if people have responded but don't show up, the money on food has been wasted. The topic of RSVPs will reemerge throughout the book because they influence so many elements.

Remember, one of the primary purposes of this book is to educate you on what vendors want you to know before you even consult with them. Vendors have your best interest at heart, and they can become your new friends along the way! Assumptions about vendors' services can be costly and can completely change your options and wedding expenses. Things are different from when your mother or even your sister planned a wedding. Knowledge and creativity are powerful and comforting tools. Accomplish your elements with some creativity to substantially reduce your costs, and it can still look great. Killing two or more birds with one stone saves money, and no birds of any feather have been harmed in the process.

**What you don't know can hurt you.** Allocating money for wedding planning is not an everyday task, so don't beat yourself up for not knowing how best to proceed. An average wedding employs fourteen to sixteen vendors, many of whom you never thought about until now. To save money, determine your priorities. And know that hiring people with little experience may cost you big time later. Be aware of items you already have on hand that you don't have to purchase or pay for. The saying, "Something old, something new, something borrowed, something blue," is more truth than poetry when it comes to saving on your wedding expenses.

**Indecision.** Beware of indecision! Indecision can make you say, "It's okay," then later wish you had opted for something else. Indecision comes from not knowing where to start. I call it "perfection paralysis." Ironically, some people elope, even though it might not be what they look back on as anything close to perfect!

If you tend be indecisive (and even if you don't), keep your receipts and don't sign large contracts until you are certain. For instance, if you change your mind on a venue, caterer, photographer, or planner after you've signed a contract, don't expect to get your retainer fee back. A retainer is not a deposit. Retainers are non-refundable, because they lock in a date for you that doesn't allow them to book anyone else for your wedding day. There are no waiting lists for wedding dates. Know up front if what you pay to a vendor is a retainer or a deposit.

Some people pretend that they are cancelling a wedding when, really, they have only changed their mind on a venue, or they've decided to elope instead. Wedding vendors tend to know what is a real-life emergency, and we know that it is better to cancel a wedding than to enter a marriage that has some big question marks hanging over it. It's important for you to distinguish between a bit of nervousness and something bigger. There's never a more important time to listen to your gut feeling. If you do back out of a wedding, some vendors will let you apply the retainer fee when you find the real Mr. or Ms. Right, especially if they can book that date again. Things happen, and we understand.

I thrive on helping indecisive couples find their starting point and ushering them from dread to excitement. My reward comes from knowing that everything will be great, will reflect their personalities, and will cost less than they might have thought. It's all about creating enjoyable memories—your memories!

**Dishonesty.** I hate to say it, but there are people who try to pass off a wedding as if it were a completely different event, thinking that will save them money. For example, they tell a DJ that they're planning a child's birthday party, thinking that will be less costly than a wedding. But they get exactly what they pay for—service suitable for a child's birthday party. It's like comparing grasshoppers to elephants. These events are vastly different in the amount of preparation, consultations, and communication required. People who request services under false pretenses will not get the services they desire. Not even close. Be honest with your vendor. Be courteous and truthful. Communication is the key.

**Choose a theme.** Theme starts with the venue you choose. If you like a rustic setting, then a venue with marble floors and crystal chandeliers won't feel right for you. The right venue that lends itself to your style will inherently contribute to your design or theme. Choosing a venue that screams your theme will save money on decorating. Adapting a marble and crystal chandelier venue for a rustic forest theme is costly, labor intensive, and unsatisfying (at best). Choose your venue and theme carefully. It's your opportunity to express your story and personalities on your special day.

**Don't go overboard.** Setting a theme will guide you through your decorating as well as the bigger aspects for your wedding and reception, and it will minimize distractions. Some of those distracting "squirrels" are tempting and darn cute, but think of them as rodents when it comes to staying within your budget. Purchasing anything and everything that fits your theme can spell disaster for your budget and storage and can make the setup time at your wedding more confusing. You don't need a sparse or boring theme, but too much of a good thing can become problematic. If you love the whimsical, chaotic, or eccentric look, go for it! Just ask yourself why you're buying each particular item. Go sparingly on the "because it fits with the theme," unless you will not be able to get it out of your mind and are scared that it won't be there another day.

**Dual purposing.** Sometimes a small budget sweats incredible genius. This is especially true when you envision what you want and know that you can't afford it all. Create or purchase items that can serve a dual purpose. Think of cupcakes arranged as your centerpiece *and* your wedding cake. Put bridesmaids' bouquets (and your bouquet) into vases and use them to decorate the head table. The flowers will thank you for it! If you want, knock out favors, table decorations, and place cards with one punch. There are a million things that you can do that serve more than one purpose and reduce costs. For example, place cards for the guest's table can be decorative and can also be used as a favor. Instead of slicing cake for the guests, serve cupcakes, to be picked up at the escort card table. Or simply have the cupcakes at the tables as place cards. For hot-weather events, make your programs into a fan and attach them to a stick.

Any decorative items that are edible will minimize post-reception cleanup. Make your favors easy to consume or take home. Be mindful that containers with water might spill in the car on the way home. Chocolate is almost always a winner. Calculate the cost of materials and add it to the cost of your labor in dollars multiplied by the number of hours to figure out the actual expense. M + (L x H) = Total Cost

**Pleasing Them.** *They* say you're supposed to do this or that. Who in the heck are *They*? *They* are not friends of independent thinking, that's for sure! Usually, the spokesperson for *Them* is a friend or relative with an idea that someone grabbed out of the sky, well-meaning or not. If you do not care one iota about having a wedding cake, don't have a wedding cake. You can do donuts, caramel corn, brownies, or whatever your heart desires that is non-traditional but still yummy. If you hate aisle runners, don't have one.

Some venues don't even allow them. If you hate flowers, wear and carry something else. There are tons of ideas using fabric, ribbon, feathers, buttons, etc. I personally would love to carry beautiful double-scoop ice cream cones instead! I've never seen this done, but in the right setting it could be fun. Be your own unique self. Don't let *Them* bust your budget or morale.

**Wedding Planner as a resource.** People tend to choose what is familiar. When everyone chooses the same venue or vendor, demand makes the price go up. I'm not saying you should go with inexperienced vendors. Never! But if a person or place is in high demand, their price may not fit your budget. Venues that are new on the scene are hungry for business. As a Wedding Planner, I loved connecting my clients with the new venues that were pleading for business and saving them money in the process. New venues seek out Wedding Planners to help bring clients. That means a Wedding Planner is a good resource to find an affordable venue.

**Research the fees.** In your Visionnaire exercise, you set your priorities. Choose items within your price range as they relate to your priority list. That said, we all know that cheap can be costly in the long run if low price means low quality. As you read on, you might change your mind about vendor categories that you want to add.

**Time it right.** Flowers or food that can't be sourced locally or within the country cost more. If flowers are a priority for your wedding and you know which flowers you want, think about that when selecting your wedding date. Flowers in season are less expensive. The same applies to food. Locally sourced products cost less.

If you love roses, don't set your date during Valentine's week. Logistics make roses expensive. A crop must be destroyed the summer before Valentine's Day and replaced with roses so that they can be harvested at just the right time, shipped, flown, and delivered all over the world for one specific day of the year. All those related businesses have to hire a lot more people for that season than they normally employ. It's all hands on deck! Thus, roses cost more around Valentine's Day.

Long engagements also add to your costs. Shorter engagements inherently help you focus on what you want and want you need. You don't have as much time to browse before purchasing. If you have a clear vision and are willing to dedicate and use your time frugally, you will not be distracted by squirrels. If it makes you feel like you're in a pressure cooker, allow for a longer engagement. If getting married sooner feels important, you can accomplish amazing things in a short period of time.

In summary, make your money and time work for you and your priorities. Be creative and don't listen to *Them*.

# 3

⟡⟡⟡⟡⟡⟡⟡⟡⟡⟡⟡⟡⟡⟡⟡⟡⟡⟡⟡⟡⟡⟡⟡

# Plan Your
# Honeymoon First

"So, when's the big day?" This is one of the first questions you will be asked. It's okay to say you haven't chosen a date yet. There's a lot of "what comes first, the chicken or the egg?" in wedding planning. You can't just pick a date out of the blue without expecting some complications.

Most people don't realize how their wedding date affects their budget. Busy seasons and off-seasons for weddings vary from region to region. Usually they are related to the weather and what people consider to be a nice time of the year. Undoubtedly, off-season rates for venues are much lower, as are mid-week rates. You have hit the jackpot if you catch both scenarios for the wedding and the honeymoon during off-season times.

This next revelation usually floors people: If you want a honeymoon right after the wedding, you should plan the wedding date around the honeymoon. Why in the world would you do that? Because modes of travel and destinations will have the greatest price fluctuations of almost any other element in your total wedding event.

An independent travel agent can tell you about discounts and upgrades, quickly respond to your questions, and be your point of contact if you have a bad experience. A travel agent will listen to what you want and tell you if it is within your budget. If a particular location doesn't fit your budget, they can suggest other places that offer similar experiences. Taking advantage of off-season rates and times when a destination is least popular can save you a bundle of money. An off-season wedding and off-season honeymoon can be less expensive, and it doesn't mean you'll have bad weather for any of it.

Some people choose a date that will be easy to remember for future anniversaries. This might be sentimental, but what if that decision drastically increases the cost of your wedding? It's an individual decision, but you might want to decide what elements are important for your wedding. Can you choose a date that is memorable that coincides with a less expensive season? Let's say that you love hydrangeas. Depending upon the time of the year, it's going to be really difficult to quench the hydrangeas' thirst. One hour out of water and they are gone. A flower that is in season or doesn't have to be shipped from out of the country will save you money. Decide if your priorities fit well for the date that you choose.

Okay, you don't have to sacrifice all of the romance in choosing your wedding date. However, there are things to be aware of that you might have not have considered. Much of this relates to your venue location. What kind of events might you be competing against at or near the venue? Some things you just can't predict. I planned one wedding that almost got interrupted by a Little League Baseball parade at a public park. When the venue was reserved, there was no way to know that the little guys would win the championship. Their parade took place within hours of the wedding—close enough to give us a little scare, but everything turned out fine.

In another story, on rehearsal day at that park near the tennis courts, we were testing the sound system at the amphitheater when a police car drove up. The policeman said that two elderly ladies at the tennis courts had reported that there were teenagers "over here" smoking pot and making noise. When he discovered what was really happening, he said, "You're definitely not a teenager!" (Did he really have to say it that way?) We definitely were not smoking pot! You never know what will cause a funny wedding memory.

Do you want your anniversary to be on the same day as someone else's? I've known friends could not attend each other's weddings because they unknowingly chose the same wedding date. That happens when weddings are scheduled during peak season. On the bright side, you can celebrate your anniversaries together.

Many people choose birthdays for their wedding date. How will that feel a few years down the road? Will you feel cheated if your birthday and anniversary get bunched into one event? Missed gifts aside, resentment can build from the sensation that each event didn't merit its own special day. That's more important to some people than to others.

Weather can be a determining factor in choosing your wedding date. Weather is fickle just about anywhere. In the Pacific Northwest, couples schedule summer weddings hoping to avoid rain. It often rains anyway. In Seattle, we are like moles squinting in the sunlight in the summer. People who are not used to the heat, will be miserable in the long-awaited sunshine. Plan B is as important as Plan A. I think it's safe not to worry about the weather. Instead, get a venue that can accommodate an indoor or an outdoor wedding, or have an outdoor wedding with a tent without sidewalls so people can be out of the rain or get some relief from the heat. The silver lining about cloudy skies is they make for great photos.

Some people choose Holidays, thinking the extra day added to a weekend is a benefit for their guests. In reality, travel and lodging rates are higher, and there's more traffic on the road. This can result in late arrivals. If guests don't mind coming in a day early and they leave plenty of time to fight local traffic, it's not so much of a problem.

Speaking of traffic, check with your local or state government and see when and where construction projects are scheduled around the time of your wedding. It's a way to show appreciation to your guests when you can offer alternate routes. Speaking of construction, when you consider choosing your wedding date at a particular venue, be sure they won't be in the middle of a remodeling project that will detract from your event.

Picking a date doesn't have to be difficult, as long as you prepare for potential obstacles. An ounce of preparation is worth a pound of peace.

While your wedding day is just one of 365 days in a year, it's almost guaranteed to have more elements and moving parts than any other day in your life. The universe doesn't play favorites to weddings, and anything that can happen on an ordinary day can happen on your wedding day. The more you can go with the flow and keep it simple, the more you will be free to soak in the memories. You, the couple, set the tone of the wedding. If you are in a frenzy from poor planning, everyone at your wedding will feel the frenzy. If you are easy-going, your guests will pick up on that and enjoy the occasion.

**Pick a wedding date that feels right for you**. Accept the fact that not everyone will be able to attend. Technology gives you options to accommodate people even if they can't be there. Ask a videographer about live streaming your wedding. Let the weather be a happy storm! At the end of the day you will be married, no matter what!

# 4

✧◇✧◇◇◇◇◇◇◇◇◇◇◇◇◇◇◇◇◇◇◇◇◇✧

# Honeymoons,
# Destination Weddings,
# & Out-of-Town Guests

**Travel agents—don't leave home without one.** Sometimes, the least expensive way of doing something makes a wedding more expensive. This is especially true when it comes to travel plans. A travel agent is indispensable to help you get the best honeymoon you can buy and leave you more money to spend on what's most important to you. Contact a travel agent six to eight months before the wedding and honeymoon, but no more than a year before. As with all wedding vendors, communication is critical.

Whether you have a destination wedding or a local one with out-of-town guests, a travel agent can help. You won't regret it, and eliminating stress is priceless. Your consultation fee will include tailoring your honeymoon package as well as your guests' travel needs. Your agent can make the hotel and travel arrangements for your guests and be the contact person if they have any problems. The biggest benefit is that you don't need to be relaying travel information to people while you're busy doing a million other things. Your guests can present their questions to your travel agent, and that contact person will set their minds at ease.

**Room blocks.** Your guests will save money if they coordinate with your travel agent, whether you have a destination wedding or not. Your agent can reserve a room block to save your guests money. When enough rooms (usually a minimum of ten) are needed, it qualifies for a hotel discount. Your guests can also get special excursion discounts, amenities, or access to events in your name when they go through your independent travel agent. Your agent will know of shuttles or other transportation options for your guests. Those guests who don't participate in the room block may miss out on enjoyable events, especially with destination weddings. Non-participants' names won't be on the list for, say, a special private cocktail event or a visit to a local attraction at a discount rate. Destination weddings offer guests a mini-vacation and a good time. No one can accomplish this like a travel agent.

**Meet in person.** If you are planning a destination wedding or a honeymoon, schedule an in-person consultation to exchange information and ideas with your travel agent. They will get to know you and show you ideas you might not have considered. You can also converse electronically, but who doesn't like to physically thumb through a brochure and share excitement over a new idea? When you're in the same room, your travel agent knows exactly what you are looking at. You can count on seeing attractions you never knew existed, even in your own backyard! After the initial consultation, you can communicate any changes or ideas by email.

What if you have your heart set on a destination that you can't afford? A travel agent can pinpoint your dream destinations and activities, especially the pricier ones, and then translate those "ideals" into affordable options for you. Your travel agent won't refer you to a decrepit dive of a hotel. If you have problems with a location, rental, or an experience, your agent will help you out of an awkward situation.

**Honeymoon registries and charities.** Couples are getting married at an older age now. They have all of the household goods they need. What they don't have is time or extra money, and they often enjoy experiences more than material possessions. If you're in this group, honeymoon registries are a perfect solution. Instead of gifts, your guests can put money towards a nice dinner, a local scuba diving adventure, or complimentary drinks at the hotel bar. It's a privilege for guests to contribute experiences that a couple might not be able to enjoy again for years, as added responsibilities complicate their lives. People who can't make it to your wedding will enjoy contributing to a memorable honeymoon for you. Ask your travel agent about their partnerships with honeymoon registries.

Another alternative for those who would rather not receive gifts is to suggest a charity to support in the name of the couple.

# 2

## The Where and Weather

# 1

## Space—Your First Frontier!

It might seem obvious, but it is best to make an appointment to check out venues rather than dropping in unannounced. Take notes, because as you ask questions, other questions will pop up. Many things don't immediately meet the eye when it comes to choosing your venue. Knowledge is power, and it can prevent headaches later in your planning process.

---

*Beware: When an item, amenity, or service*
*is "provided," it is not necessarily free.*

---

For example, when a venue says they provide linens, that may mean they carry an inventory of linens, which are available for a fee. When you hear the word "provide," ask what it means, so you don't wallow in regret later.

# QUESTIONS TO ASK ABOUT THE VENUE

## General:

1.  Is the venue available for our wedding date?

2.  What time can we access the venue on the wedding day to get ready?

3.  When do we have to be out of the venue?

4.  What if we need extra time?

5.  If we exceed our rental time, what will happen?

6.  Is the space big enough to accommodate our guest count for our wedding and reception?

7.  If the space is not big enough without a transition *(called a flip)* between the wedding and reception, is there space for a cocktail hour to accommodate our guests during the transition?

8.  Is there a designated room for the wedding party to get dressed and do hair and makeup?

## Deposits and Retainers:

1.  What is the price for the venue space?

2.  How much is the retainer fee to reserve our date?

3.  When is the retainer fee due?

4.  When is the final payment due?

5.  How much is the damage deposit?

6.  Do you keep a credit card on file and only use it if there is damage?

7.  Will someone do a walkthrough with us to document any existing damage so that we don't get charged for it?

8.  Will someone do a walkthrough with us or someone we trust for after the wedding to make sure any damages are documented correctly?

9.  Can we have a pet participate in the ceremony? If so, what are the rules?

## Deadlines:

1. (If the venue provides catering) When do you need a preliminary guest count?

2. When do you need a final guest count?

## Capacity:

1. What is the maximum number of people allowed in the reception room for the following styles of dinners? Which style takes the least time?

- Plated
- Buffet
- Family style
- Reception style ("reception style" means standing only, with a few cocktail tables)

2. How is the room's use and capacity determined? Is it within the International Code Council adhered to by the fire department?

## Placement of Specific Items:

- Dance floor
- DJ/emcee
- Guestbook
- Dessert station/candy buffet
- Head table
- Gift table
- Wedding cake table
- Sweetheart table
- Coat check

## Rehearsals:

1. Can we have our rehearsal here?

2. Can we use the room we're reserving for our rehearsal?

3. If not, is there another area onsite where we can have a rehearsal?

4. How long do we have for a rehearsal?

5. Is there an extra charge for a rehearsal?

6. What day of the week do you usually have rehearsals?

## Facility Conditions and Amenities:

1. Will there be any remodeling projects around the time of our wedding?

2. Are bathrooms and entrances near the reception room handicapped accessible?

## What the Rental Fee Includes:

1. Tables? If so, what sizes and shapes?

2. Chairs? If so, what style, size, etc.?

3. Do the chairs need covers? If so, are they provided and is there a fee?

4. If chair covers are not included, can you recommend a rental company that has them to fit the chairs?

## Onsite catering:

1. Do you have a food and beverage minimum?

2. If we meet the food and beverage minimum, are the room fees or any other fees waived?

3. When do you need the preliminary and final guest counts?

4. What is your policy on food being packaged to take home after the event?

5. Do you provide a basket or box for a small meal for us when we get back to our room?

6. Will someone on staff cut the cake? If so, is there a fee?

8. Is there refrigeration, so the pastry chef can deliver the cake early?

9. If the temperature is cool enough, do you set up the cake table first so the pastry chef can deliver it early?

10. Do you allow offsite caterers (especially important for ethnic cuisine)?

## Linens/Rentals for Reception:

*(If the venue does not provide onsite catering, ask these same questions of catering or rental companies that you interview.)*

Are any of the following included in the rental fee? If so, what colors/styles are included:

- Tablecloths
- Overlays
- Runners
- Plates
- Glassware
- Stemware
- Cutlery

## Bartending:

1. Is an onsite bartender available, or do we need to hire a professional bartender who is properly licensed and insured?

2. Do we need a permit to serve alcohol?

3. Do we have to provide our own alcohol?

4. Do you require event insurance, no matter who provides the alcohol?

5. Can we have signature drinks for toasting? Do you provide non-alcoholic options?

6. What is your policy for open bars and cash bars?

7. What is the cost if you provide the alcohol?

## Audio/Visual Equipment:

1. Do you provide a sound system for music? If so, is there a fee? (DJs generally avoid in-house sound systems, because they usually are designed for speaking and not for music.)

2. How loud can the music be inside the venue?

4. How old is the sound system?

5. What types of microphones are included (wireless handheld, lapel, corded in a mic stand, battery pack, earpiece, headset, mic in lectern)?

7. Do you put fresh batteries in them for every event?

8. Can we play a slideshow or video presentation for the wedding or reception?

9. What types of presentations are common in the event space?

10. Can you provide the name of a DJ who has done weddings here? (Ask prior DJs about their experience. If you have a professional Wedding Planner, she might already know and have current information about the venue's sound system.)

11. Do you provide or rent a dance floor?

12. If so, how large is it?

13. What does it cost, if it isn't included in the venue rental fee?


## Lodging:

1. Is lodging available onsite? If so, do you provide room blocks so our guests can get a lower rate?

2. If lodging is not available onsite, do you have a working relationship with local hotels?

2. What local hotels provide room blocks so that our guests can get a lower rate?

3. Do those hotels have a shuttle service to and from the venue?

## Decorating:

1. How early can we come in to decorate?

2. Can we attach anything to the walls? If so, with what? (Generally no tape, nails, tacks, or adhesives are allowed.)

3. Can we use helium balloons? (Often, no balloons of any type are allowed, because if they escape to the ceiling, they can set off the sprinkler system.)

4. If no helium balloons, can we use regular balloons?

5. Can we use bubbles?

6. Can we use real rose petals? (Maybe not, as they can leave stains.)

7. Can we use artificial rose petals? (Maybe not, as they can cause a slip hazard.)

8. Can we use glitter?

9. Can we use confetti?

10. Can we have candles? If so, what types of candles?

11. Can we have a sparkler send-off outdoors?

12. If other clients have donated decorations, are they available for our use?

13. Can we have an aisle runner?

## Parking:

1. Is there street parking?

2. Is there a paid parking garage or lot?

3. Is valet parking available? If so, it is exclusive or optional?

4. Is parking validated?

## Security:

1. Is there a secure place away from the door for gifts and cards?

2. Can the guest book be placed well inside the room to keep information confidential and our items from being stolen?

3. Is there security staff in the parking area?

4. If a guest is unruly, how can we contact security?

## Signage:

1. Where are signs placed to direct traffic to the venue?

2. Will there be signage directing people where to park?

3. Will there be directions from the parking lot to the specific event space in the building?

4. What kind of signage is next to the room for our wedding/reception?

## Communication:

1. Who can I contact after hours or on weekends for crucial updates or emergencies?

2. Who can I contact after hours during the week for crucial updates or emergencies?

## Preferred Vendors:

1. Do you have a preferred vendor list?

2. Do I have to use the vendors on your list, or can I use other professional vendors?

3. If you make exceptions, how do I get them approved?

# NOTES:

# 2

## A Place to Remember

The venue is your wedding's home for the day. No matter why you choose a particular venue, you will remember it for years to come. So, tend to the details to support those memories. Planning is key! No two venues are alike, even though they accomplish pretty much the same thing. That's good! You will find the environment that has your wedding written all over it.

**Location, location, location.** Finding a venue is like house hunting. I feel like a real estate agent when I'm showing clients potential venues that match their vision of what they want. I point out features that might be of concern or might be a huge plus. The questions are automatic for me, but I'm always pleased when a client feels relief in the process. I often hear, "Thanks for asking the questions I'm afraid to ask!"

You'll know when you have found what feels like "home" to you, when you can't get it out of your mind and you imagine your vision coming to life there. You know when the wedding dress is right, because you don't want to take it off. You know when the venue is right, because you don't want to leave. Often, finding a venue and finding the wedding dress happen almost simultaneously. A bride-to-be, might have envisioned the dress and venue—maybe for years!

A wedding venue might be your wedding's home for the day, but the people who own it know every nook and cranny. They know what works best and the reason behind placing things in certain places. They know where it's best not to place something at certain times of the day. They have hosted countless events and weddings there, and they want your day to go as smoothly as you do!

**Communicate, communicate, communicate.** A smooth wedding results from good communication of your vision with the venue coordinator. Once you have booked a venue, promptly communicate any changes, second thoughts, or new ideas that arise. Ask the questions you wish you had asked the them at your previous site visit. They will listen and do their best to accommodate your new idea, but if there is something in your vision that you might regret, they are there to tell you that, too.

**Explore the options.** Know what options venues offer. Check the rates for different packages. Sometimes the guest count or the day of the week can reduce the cost. If you need more hours, check for any per-hour packages. Ask questions and communicate every detail you can think of to keep you all on the same page.

**Food and drink.** Never bring alcohol in addition to what a bartender has coordinated with you to have available. Alcohol must be kept secure. And don't bring outside food to a catered event. Caterers risk the consequences for food poisoning, even from food they haven't prepared. The potential risk for bartenders is even greater. Venues are not licensed to serve alcohol; bartenders are. Venues and unplanned alcohol do not mix.

Bartenders keep the inventory safe during and after the wedding. They know how much alcohol and what types you will need to order for the number of guests you have. They look for signs of intoxication from the moment the first drink is served.

Your venue will likely require event insurance, even if only for the fact that alcohol is being served. Explore this option: www.WedSafe.com.

**A peek behind the venue scenes.** Your venue is one of your largest wedding investments. The before and after work and expenses for your venue owner and venue coordinator are like the underwater part of an iceberg. You may never see them. And just because they service hundreds or thousands of people every year, that doesn't mean they don't care as much about your wedding as they do other events. As a Wedding Planner, I have experienced only a sample of the cleanup: folding and stacking tables and chairs, removing decorations and linens, sweeping the floor, and dealing with items left behind by guests—and that's just indoors. Add a yard or some acreage to that, and your hourly rate for the ambience you love is a bargain! The size of the property doesn't necessarily dictate the price, but it generates some of the hidden efforts to make your wedding day a happy memory.

**The best venue experience.** Some couples are so focused on their own experience, they forget to consider their guests.

1. Know the various ages of your guests and offer something that makes them excited, nostalgic, or in awe.

2. Some guests won't have been to a wedding in decades, and things have changed.

3. Do your guests know what to expect next?

4. Will they have a clue what the shoe game is? A good DJ helps with all of your guests' experience.

5. Signage or other printed information at the guest tables will keep your guests in the know.

6. Guests from different cultures will especially appreciate helpful hints and information.

Both you and your venue can benefit greatly if you hire a day-of coordinator. There are too many moving parts to delegate everything to friends or family. In fact, you will enjoy your day more when your friends and family can enjoy every moment of your celebration rather than working during those once-in-a lifetime moments.

**Why it costs so much.** Alcohol is a significant factor in venue cost. Do yourself a huge favor by hiring a professional bartending service. They can keep people in check, and that's a requirement for two reasons:

First, alcohol consumption at a wedding exponentially increases the risk of damage to a venue. Sometimes the damage isn't limited to property. Depending on the location, you might need a permit to serve alcohol.

Second, in the last few years, industry professionals and venue owners have connected to figure out how to deal with clients, families, and guests who are discourteous or disrespectful. Alcohol compounds the problem and can turn discourteous people unbearable or downright dangerous. Some professionals simply charge more to accommodate for unwanted behavior. Sometimes added security is needed. I've seen it with my own eyes more than once, and it nearly made me back out of the wedding planning profession!

**Payment.** You will need to pay a retainer to reserve your date. Beyond that, venue payment schedules vary. Mark the payment deadlines on your calendar. If not fully paid on time, the venue has the right to lock all its gates and doors, and no one wants that to happen. Expect a receipt for all of your payments. If you don't get one, contact the venue to be sure there's not a problem. Again, planning and communication are key to a fantastic wedding day!

You may also pay damage deposits that can be returned partially or in full, depending upon any damage from your group. Your credit card will be on file in case damages occur beyond what the deposit covers. Prevent an unpleasant surprise by doing a walkthrough on the day of your wedding or at the rehearsal, if it is the day before the wedding. The venue should have a checklist of key items to consider, much like the once-over form used by rental car companies. Plan for this or insist on it. A professional Wedding Planner can ease your duties by doing both the pre-event and post-event walkthrough. Also, check out the options available through wedding insurance. Check out <u>WedSafe.com</u>.

# 3

◇◇◇◇◇◇◇◇◇◇◇◇◇◇◇◇◇◇◇◇◇◇◇◇◇◇◇◇

## Backyard Weddings

People often think backyard weddings will save them venue fees. You may have sentimental reasons to get married in a particular backyard. Maybe you love the view or the ambience, or you grew up there and always envisioned your perfect wedding there. Maybe a friend or relative has actually volunteered their space as a wedding gift to you.

A backyard wedding isn't as simple as you might think. The hosts' home is their castle, whether or not they've cared for it as such. Commitment to hosting a wedding brings up the to-do list they've been avoiding for years. I know some people who actually replaced a roof that wasn't due to be replaced, just because they were hosting a large family event. People can go a little crazy—way beyond tidying up the house before last-minute guests arrive. They will paint, re-carpet, remodel the guest bedroom, or refurbish the landscape. They might even build a new doghouse, if they think it will look better. Does this feel like stress? Telling them not to worry won't keep them from exceeding their budget or doing back-breaking work. Weigh all of these things when you consider a backyard wedding.

**The loo, privy, john, or lav.** Most backyards aren't designed to host 150 people for a wedding. Things that automatically come with a regular venue, hotel, or a church aren't available on residential property. Let's get real. It's not fair to expect the homeowners to allow people inside to use the bathroom (with possible exceptions to accommodate elderly or handicapped guests). Sewer or septic systems are not meant to accommodate 150 house guests in a single day. The alternative is to provide one or more outdoor toilets, delivered on a flatbed truck. And if same-day delivery isn't possible, the homeowners (and their neighbors) get to enjoy that architectural wonder for days on end. The up side is that some of the nicer ones have air conditioning, piped-in music, flushable toilets, and even art on the walls. Some units are handicapped accessible, and some fancier ones even come with showers. They can easily become the talk of your wedding. Check out RoyalRestrooms.com.

Just for fun, research the hilarious names that are chosen for these types of services. But, seriously—people will likely be wearing nicer clothes. Will they be comfortable in their finest attire in a typical outdoor toilet?

I love helping my clients during the week before the wedding, so they can welcome their friends and family, instead of scurrying around tending to logistics. Tents and dance floors can't all be delivered on the day of the wedding, and I can be the one to make sure that everything is placed correctly. It's satisfying to free up the couples' time by picking up linens, waiting at an outdoor venue two days ahead of time while a portable outdoor restroom is being delivered, and keeping the keys safe until the wedding. The life of a Wedding Planner isn't glamorous! But I do have fun making "Reserved for the Jones wedding on Saturday" signs for the doors of the portable restrooms. Some couples feature those signs in their wedding pictures!

**A wonderful day in the neighborhood?** The eyesore of portable restrooms aside, here's a way to know what a host's neighbors are really like: Ask if it's okay for people to park in front of their house. It's good to know if the neighbors will put the gracious hosts through a version of hell prior to and on the wedding day.

And don't be surprised if more than one wedding occurs within a single block, especially on lakefront property. I've seen it firsthand. When you hear someone else's processional music as you are beginning the setup, you thank your lucky stars that your receptions won't be clashing with each other to irritate the entire neighborhood.

Most neighborhoods or cities have codes about how loud the music can be (measured in decibels) and how late the music can be played. Don't take this issue lightly. A wedding is the last place you want to have cops show up at the door. It takes the romance right out of the day. To minimize neighborhood traffic, consider hiring a shuttle to transport your guests to and from the wedding from a pre-approved parking lot. Find a park-and-ride lot that's not so busy on weekends. For a small fee, you might be able to use a nearby school's parking lot.

**Don't assume.** Did you know that venues with onsite catering sometimes offer the space without fee if a minimum amount of food is ordered? Free venue space plus onsite catering is nothing to dismiss when you're planning a wedding. This might make it possible to invite more guests.

Before you decide on a backyard wedding, figure out the extra costs involved. If cost is your concern, you may save money by using a regular venue. Rentals for tables, chairs, dance floor, tent, and restrooms will be more for a backyard wedding. Depending upon the number of guests and style of your reception, you may also need to rent tablecloths and linens, plates, stemware, and cutlery. Many or all of these are included in the price of a venue with onsite catering. Backyard weddings are beautiful and sentimental, but weigh other factors before you decide.

When the economy crashed in 2008, many couples wanted to keep their wedding budgets trim. Often, their first thought was to bypass the usual wedding venues, including hotels. The AIG (American International Group) received bad press in 2009 for how they allocated money received from the bailout by Congress. The reports that they had spent money in the multiple six figures on travel for just a few employees were inaccurate. In reality, these employees had been recognized at a conference, and their expenses were paid for by those hosting the event. Nonetheless, that story caused a storm of cancellations from corporations not wanting to get bad press for spending money on conferences and on down the line. This hurt the hospitality industry severely. As a result, many venues that previously catered to corporate business and had snubbed their noses at social events (like weddings), were suddenly begging for the social event market. They created packages to attract weddings. It pained me to hear of people making expensive choices, when they could have had some screaming deals from hotels. Couples were finding backyard weddings to be more expensive than they anticipated. During that time, I also found venues that were new on the scene. My clients who used these venues saved hundreds of dollars and more. Whether or not the economy crashes, check out the venues that will be hungry for your business before you assume that a backyard wedding is less expensive.

All that said, some of the best and favorite weddings I planned were hosted in backyards with breathtaking views. They have an extra set of challenges, but the pictures are phenomenal, and everyone has a great time in an outdoor setting.

# 4

<><><><><><><><><><><><><><><><><><><><><><>

# Weather, Tents,
# and Backup Plans

**It's elemental.** A backyard has no roof. Clouds and the sun are a given, and either or both can drench or burn people's skin. Smart weddings are often Plan B weddings that include a plan for shelter in case of rain or unbearable heat from the sun. Renting a tent from a party rental store is the best option, but they are in high demand during the busy wedding season. If you want to reserve a tent, plan several months ahead. Within a few days of the wedding you should have a good idea whether or not you'll actually need the tent, and you have the option to cancel the order.

You can't melt your wedding cake and eat it, too. A wedding cake is not meant to be out in the heat, and it needs to be sheltered. The Leaning Tower of Pisa isn't most people's idea for the design of their wedding cake, but that's what they get when heat has its way. With so much else going on, you don't want to worry about propping up a cake. Designate a special place that can adequately cool the cake and ask a caterer or other experienced person to move the cake outside at the appropriate time. Make sure the cake table is ready and waiting for the cake to land. There's even a phone app to help you know if the cake table is level.

Remember that there needs to be adequate space, amenities, and shelter for caterers, wait staff, and a DJ. Vendors need easy access to electrical outlets, water, and restrooms. They need shelter if the weather is inclement or too hot. Don't risk ruining music and sound equipment to the tune of thousands of dollars. ALWAYS protect your DJ! He or she will appreciate an appointment to look at the overall setting and the layout you have planned for the site design. A Wedding Planner (if you have one) can meet your vendors onsite after you've decided on the layout. You want to know how much space each vendor requires and how much room is left for guests. Some vendors will be making deliveries on the wedding day, and they need good access. Don't make them navigate a maze.

**Is a backyard wedding the best option?** Weather is one of the biggest factors couples take into account when choosing a wedding date. It's a game of chance, at best. There are options to make that a non-issue, and those options include backup Plan B or C or D. Tents are a must for outdoor weddings if the wedding can't be moved indoors. Even if you are pretty certain of the weather, not all of your guests will necessarily be comfortable. A tent solves the problem, and no one will be upset if for most of the day you don't need one. On the other hand, if someone is the tiniest bit miserable they will remember it always!

In an area with a mild climate, even when the sun comes out, people act like moles coming out of the ground, squinting in discomfort. If it gets below 50 degrees Fahrenheit, people shiver. Tents can be the answer for either extreme. People from different parts of the country are acclimated to different conditions. Shelter is a basic need. Consider Goldilocks, testing all three of the bears' porridge. Only a third of the porridge felt just right. Same goes for the weather and comfort level for everyone. Erring on the side of caution pays off.

**Tents and canopies.** Tents get a bad rap. But some very elegant venues use them, and they can be beautiful. A "canopy"—a unit consisting of only the legs and the roof—may be less expensive. On the other hand, some vendors charge the same, with or without sidewalls. Research and compare products and pricing. Side panels and leg wraps (coverings for poles supporting the tent) can add to the costs of materials and labor. With either a tent or a canopy, you can ask the company to drape the ceiling and hang a chandelier for a nicer look.

Even if you think you won't need a tent for your outdoor wedding, you will be well served to pay a deposit on one. Check the policies. See how far in advance they will let you reserve or cancel an order. Don't wait until the last minute, but plan for it early on. Otherwise, just like the last-minute shoppers on Christmas Eve, the latest craze in toys will be gone. Be ready to protect your guests from getting drenched or sunburned.

Tornados are common in some parts of the country. As you can imagine, tornados aren't particularly friendly to tents. Are there underground tornado-proof wedding venues? I haven't done the research on that, but it's something to consider if you live in such a region. Different parts of the country have entirely opposite wedding seasons. In Las Vegas, forget about an outdoor wedding in the summertime. Many venues won't even allow it. In the Pacific Northwest, July through September are the most popular times for weddings. June isn't particularly popular west of the Cascade Mountains, because there is still too much chance of rain. East of the Cascades is a high desert, with totally different conditions. Bottom line, your Plan A might work, but like a Boy Scout, be prepared. (Boy Scouts use tents, too!)

Weather in general is iffy enough that Plan B should get just as much consideration as Plan A. Mother Nature couldn't care less about your wedding. Some people think that rain on a wedding day brings good luck. I know of many weddings where it was cloudy right up until the ceremony, and then the sun came out. Maybe Mother Nature has your back after all! Take whatever comes, and enjoy every minute of Plan A or Plan B or C or D.

PLANNING STAGE

# 3

## Wedding Attire

Not every bride likes to pick a dress right away. Some brides hate shopping for dresses. But keep in mind that ordering instead of choosing something off of the rack can take at least nine months just to receive it, never mind the extra time for alterations. Some brides feel good buying a dress from a charitable organization where the sales proceeds help those suffering from breast cancer, etc. Do an online search for "touring charities" to find donated dresses.

# 1

## The Wedding Dress

Before you shop for dresses, consider visiting a dressmaker/alterations specialist to see options for a custom-made gown. Bridal store dresses off the rack seldom fit an "average" bride. Sometimes, the first place people think to shop for a dress is the exact place I would never take a bride to shop. A dress from any place other than a boutique is often problematic for photographers because of the inferior quality of the fabric. An alterations specialist can spot these dresses, too. Department store dresses are made more "to alter" than "to get to the altar"—photographers spend more time editing because of the poorer quality of material. Department stores make a killing on alterations, which may be why their prices are lower. A professional with the right expertise is critical, because dresses can easily be ruined when someone doesn't know how to press or steam specialty fabrics. Just don't be deceived.

A custom-made dress requires minimal alteration. Sometimes (not always) an independent alterations specialist or seamstress can make you a dress for less money. Factors include if the dress will be designed or sewn from a pattern; what type of fabric used; number and intricacy of embellishments. Indulge in the type of shopping and design options that fit your style and personality. It's your wedding! If you do need alterations, it may be more economical to have the same person do alterations for the entire bridal party.

Boutique shopping is more relaxing and more intimate. Boutiques often have an onsite alterations specialist. Knowing their quality of work is trust-worthy is comforting. If you already have a trusted person to do everyone's alterations, don't hesitate, especially if they have experience working with wedding attire. My clients have found beautiful dresses at boutiques that look as if they cost hundreds or thousands of dollars more than what they paid. Assumptions can make your wedding dress costs soar. Check out the boutiques and be amazed.

**Line up your appointments.** More than ninety percent of the time you will need an appointment to be served at a bridal store, a boutique, and with an alterations specialist. You may need three alterations appointments: the first for fitting, the second for double-checking that everything is okay, and the third for the final fitting and payment. If you find a boutique that doesn't require an appointment and doesn't limit you to just one hour, shopping for a dress will be less stressful. Even if they require an appointment, lack of a time limit will make it relaxing.

**Who wants to shop?** "The more the merrier" is NOT true when it comes to shopping for wedding gowns. Don't make it a standing-room-only event. A trusted friend and/or family member is best, but not the groom. You can work solo with a professional, if that's what you prefer. People assume that brides love the experience of finding a dress, but some really dread the process.

Too many opinions can confuse the bride, make her experience miserable, and complicate the experience for everyone involved. Inviting half a dozen friends or relatives is a recipe for a disaster. If you love a dress and everyone turns their noses up at it, your joy is dashed. You will know you have found THE dress when you want to try it on again, you don't want to take it off, or it makes you break into tears. Don't let others dissuade you without good reason.

People's opinions are based on their individual taste. If they tell you why a different dress flatters you more, state your reasons for your choice. If your friend's opinion is valid, ask the alterations specialist about tweaking the dress to include that feature. Or there might be a perfect dress that combines the best of the two choices. Be open minded, but listen to your heart. It's YOUR dress. No one else is going to wear it!

**Leave food, beverages, and children at home.** Don't bring children or anything that can be chewed or swallowed on your shopping or alterations appointment! Children can easily ruin what might be your (or someone else's) wedding dress. Dirty hands and rambunctious or bored kids are dangerous in that setting. If you must bring the flower girl, be sure she is closely supervised at all times. Keep her appointment short. She may be a little angel, but youngsters can be easily overwhelmed with excitement.

**Rule** #1. Bridal shop employees beg you to comply with Rule #1: *Wear underwear—PLEASE!* You may be body beautiful, but there's a time and a place. I pity the shop attendants who have to deal with this more often than you might think!

Consider the height of the heel on your shoes. You will be much more comfortable on your wedding day when YOU WEAR the right shoes for you. Your feet seldom show during the wedding and reception, and it's especially important to have your shoes chosen by the time you have your dress altered. Some brides love shoes and will choose their shoes before they shop for a dress.

Do wear the support undergarments or corset (if any) that you will wear with your wedding dress. Support garments are great for any body type and are often available at your local fabric store. There's no sense in fitting a dress to a drastically different body than what you will have on your wedding day. The right fit might even save you the time and money of an alterations visit.

**Be honest, not ashamed.** Even though bridal garments have somewhat generous seams, you can ease the alterations process if you avoid losing or gaining a lot of weight between fittings. That's easier said than done, but if it does happen, make an appointment sooner than later. The final fitting should be relatively close to the wedding day. Know how close to the wedding date your alterations specialist wants to see you. If you are pregnant, let the alterations specialist know! If you are uncomfortable about that little announcement, make an appointment when you can be by yourself.

**The custom dress.** Dressmakers can make plus-sized women feel as beautiful as any other bride, but the bride isn't the only one who benefits. It's not always cheaper to buy a dress off the rack. A custom dress won't give you the advantages of cheap labor from another country, but you will be supporting the local economy and have a dress that is totally you! Help your seamstress by knowing what you want. If you want embellishments, purchase them, rather than expecting the dressmaker to read your mind. If you see a sewing pattern that you like, they can work with that to design a dress. Pictures with details are good, too.

**Do the bustle!** Most dresses have some sort of train built into the them. However, not all wedding dresses bought off the rack have bustles built in, or they go to the other extreme and put in way too many attachments to create a bustle. The bustle brings the length of the train up to the same level of the rest of the dress or just slightly touching the floor. A bustled dress can help prevent you and your dance partner from tripping. You need a bustle if you have a train, unless you want to hold your train with your pinky finger during the reception like someone out of a Victorian novel.

The dress is usually bustled only for the reception. The bustle should be designed to fit and look good with your dress. It will attach either on the outside or on the inside of the dress. Bustle styles vary and are often interchangeable. Study the various types of bustles online.

If your wedding dress requires sixteen ribbons to create a bustle, ask your alterations specialist reduce that number to three or four. They can be created with buttons and button loops, with hidden or covered snaps or hooks, or with ribbons underneath on the main part of the dress with another on the train or incorporated with a seam. A good alterations specialist will label each corresponding snap, hook, button, or ribbon so you won't waste time just before your reception trying to guess what attaches to what.

**Veils and headpieces.** I'll come right out and say it: Veils are the biggest rip off when you buy them at a bridal store. The materials they are made of just don't cost that much, and they aren't overly time-consuming to make. A simple veil trimmed with ribbon takes less than an hour to make if you have a sewing machine. Anyone who has crafting or sewing experience can make a veil. Head pieces take more talent, but you probably know someone who is perfectly capable of making one.

Sewing patterns for veils often include different options for lengths and types. Even buying materials and embellishments for a veil or a headpiece will save you money. Embellishments can be pricey, but even if you make a practice piece first, without the embellishments, you will not spend as much as you would buying ready-made from a store. Another option is to get a simple, less expensive craft store veil and add the embellishments or trim yourself. It's not wrong to buy a veil; just realize that you have options.

**The heirloom dress.** If you don't fit into your mother's wedding dress, join the club! That doesn't mean you can't incorporate parts of it into your dress or a ring pillow. Other than the bride's wedding, about the only time a bride's dress will be worn is when a five-year-old daughter plays dress up. Moms, if you're reading this book, don't take this personally. It's just a fact. Someone from another generation or two down the line will love wearing your dress. Vintage catches up with us and becomes fashionable.

**Preserving your dress.** It's wise to make arrangements before your wedding to preserve your wedding dress. Some companies will preserve not only your dress, but other things such as your flowers. These specialists are rare, but with enough online research you'll find someone who can create a work of art from the flowers, the dress, and other memorabilia. It goes way beyond what your dry cleaner will provide—your gown in a box. Ask your seamstress or the boutique where you buy your dress to refer you to a company that will do the type of preservation that you want.

# 2

◇◇◇◇◇◇◇◇◇◇◇◇◇◇◇◇◇◇◇◇◇◇◇◇◇◇◇◇◇◇

# Bridesmaids' Attire—
# Bring Your Shoes!

The same rules apply in shopping for the maid of honor and bridesmaids' dresses as for the bride's gown. They should wear the shoes they will wear at the wedding to ensure the right length. Another note about the shoes: If everyone will be walking on soft ground, you can get specialty caps that are to place on the heels that make a larger surface than a spiked heal. No one wants to get stuck, leave a shoe behind, break a heel, fall, or break something walking down the aisle in front of cameras.

A chain store may be a better option than a boutique for the attendants' dresses. A national chain can serve all of them with the same style number and color of dress. Look for the style number on the tag inside the dress or find it on the national chain store's website. Stick with one brand and variations of the same style number, and remember that many strapless dresses can be ordered with straps. That's an easy alteration if things don't fit properly. Perhaps you can find a bridesmaid dress in a collection that has the same look but with different bodices or lengths that complement each attendant's figure and comfort. Some people are comfortable with a halter style, some with strapless, or some with shoulder straps. It's no fun to wear something that makes you feel self-conscious.

Usually the maid/matron of honor and bridesmaids buy their own dresses and shoes, all to be coordinated, at least by color. They deserve to be comfortable. If you want all of your attendants to wear the same length dress for uniformity, let them know, and relay that information to the dress shop or your alterations specialist. For a winter wedding, the attendants might appreciate a wrap or scarf to drape over their shoulders to keep warm and the same can protect them from the heat and a sunburn in the summer.

If possible, have the same person alter all of the bridesmaids' dresses. Most independent alteration specialists will alter dresses within a few days of the wedding if your bridesmaids are flying in from another state. Some will even meet them at the airport to pick up the dress and make alterations from pictures that have been sent to them; or they will take it to their shop to be altered the next day by appointment. Plan well in advance for special alterations and final fittings for your out-of-town attendants just days before your wedding.

# 3

# Men's Formalwear

**Go local or take it national?** Once you (as a couple) have decided on colors, visit a local tuxedo shop to choose the colors for the suit or tuxedo and accent pieces to coordinate with or complement the bridesmaids' dress color. The shop will rent everything else you need except for socks and possibly kerchiefs.

Be mindful of the weather, especially for an outdoor wedding. Solid black can be sweltering in outdoor heat. If appropriate, consider a less formal look with dark or tan pants and a shirt and tie.

If three or more groomsmen rent a tuxedo from the same store, the groom may qualify for a free tuxedo. If the shop cannot accommodate the groom's size, there are tailors who design and sew men's suits and tuxedos. Plan this well in advance. Make it your first step once the bridal dress is chosen.

Better to match than clash. There are over two hundred shades of white, so check fabric samples at the wedding apparel stores.

If there isn't a tuxedo shop nearby, the groomsmen can rent their attire in person or online at a predominant men's formalwear store such as Men's Wearhouse. They carry tuxedos, suits, shoes, suspenders, vests, bow ties, neck ties, cufflinks, and cummerbunds. They sell socks and they sell the kerchiefs for suits, but for obvious reasons they don't rent them.

A national chain is great for people in different locations, because the attire will be uniform and will match. If any of the attendants (or the groom) is in the military and will be flying in only a couple days before the wedding, he can be measured at the base or relay his dress blues measurements to order (when necessary) and then pick up the formalwear. His first stop on arrival at the airport should be the formalwear store for the final fitting.

**Ordering and returning.** If the national chain carries your size, place your online order for everything you want from them at least four months prior to the wedding. Most chains have measuring guides on their website. Be sure the online orders will arrive at your home seven days in advance or at the nearest store two days before an event. For questions or concerns, call or chat with customer service. Good news, men: the waistbands are adjustable for three sizes. Formalwear options are available for boys from sizes three to eighteen. Timing for all of this can be a challenge, but with adjustable pants and excellent customer service, you won't likely be left with an emergency. Items can be returned the next day to the local store or mailed using the return label provided by the vendor.

**Your friend, the officiant.** If you have a male friend who is officiating the wedding, choose the look that you want for him. Tuxedo shops frequently have good sales. If your officiant is a friend who officiates at other weddings, he can probably purchase something in black to be used for your wedding and future weddings.

PLANNING STAGE

# 4

## Your Psychological Assistant

**Why has everyone gone nuts?** Are they messing with your psyche? Have you been told you should use unicorns for your centerpieces instead of flowers? That you must use the cake topper your sister had for her wedding last year? Maybe you want your five-year-old angel of a nephew to be your ring bearer, but your friend says if her three-year-old brat of a son doesn't fill that role, she won't attend your wedding. Side note: You can't guarantee the behavior of ring bearers or flower girls, even after rehearsals.

It's a rare and lucky person planning a wedding who doesn't hear suggestions from people they know. You'll hear everything from *I know a perfect song* to *I saw a really cool thing on TV about bridesmaid's dresses!* If you had a nickel for every tidbit of advice, you could pay for the bride's bouquet!

How do you handle the myriad of suggestions? Your best bet is silence, a nod, smile, or a simple thanks. A sense of humor goes a LONG way to get you through the wedding planning process. Suggestions thrown at you aren't sticky, and you aren't covered in Velcro, so take what you want and leave the rest. Here's what you hope not to hear—in mild, medium, and hot versions, just like salsa:

### Ideas and Questions (extra mild sauce):

1. I have a friend who did _____.

2. This is what I wish I would have done at our wedding.

3. I heard about this really cool _____!

4. Are you going to _____?

### Strong Suggestions (mild to medium sauce):

1. You should do _____!

2. This is what I would do if I were you!

3. Your Dad and I did _____ at our wedding. It would be so cool if you did that, too!

4. You're going to have the wedding I never had!

5. Who's going to be in the wedding party? Can I? Can I? Can I? Pleas-o, pleas-o, please!

**Crazy Control-Freak Suggestions (beg-for-bread hot sauce):**

1. Your Dad and I did _____ at our wedding. It would be a real shame if you didn't do _____, too!

2. I can't believe you are _____.

3. I can't believe you aren't _____.

4. What?! But it's been a TRADITION to _____!

5. How can you invite _____ and not invite _____?

6. You can't elope! I would never forgive you!

7. Remember, I'm paying for this wedding! I control the purse strings and I want this because it is kind of my wedding, too!

8. Child of mine, I never got to plan my own wedding, so now you can have the wedding I wanted!

9. That is just too weird! I don't know if I want to even be there.

10. I refuse to attend if you're inviting _____.

How do you respond to the rude or socially unacceptable darts and arrows slung in your direction? Often, the best defense is to listen in silence. Remain neutral. If you have a Wedding Planner, say that you have to talk to them first. Our job is to be a buffer, if necessary, to deliver the wedding you want.

Consider these responses to the hot-sauce remarks:

1. We've received so many suggestions that we might have to have ten weddings to incorporate everything!

2. Thanks for the idea. Can you write that down and mail it to me so I can put it in my file? (you know they won't go to all that trouble)

3. We only want to get married once, so I just don't think we'll be able to use all of these great ideas. There are sooooo many, I just can't keep my head above water!

4. We want everyone to be surprised.

5. The wedding would be paid for if I had a dollar for every idea I've heard.

6. Mom, that was great for you, but that's just not me. I hope you understand. I really would prefer not to do that. (Saying prefer is key!)

7. Mom, that was fabulous at your wedding. It made your wedding unique, all about you. I'd feel like I was stealing from you. I promise we'll do something special for you to remember, but I want it to be a surprise. (Remember to follow through on this!)

8. Thank you! That is so sweet that you care so much.

9. I'll put you at different tables so you don't have to sit near him.

10. I think I'm going to fall into a heap of tears! My brain is on overload. I hope that everyone will let me create a really cool wedding that everyone will enjoy.

Sometimes you just have to go into self-preservation mode. If you are going to meet someone for lunch who you know will do their best to drive you crazy or leave you shaking in your boots about the wedding, plan ahead. You need a support system, whether that is your Wedding Planner, Maid of Honor, or fiancé. Have them call you at mid-point with an "emergency" that you must address. Agree on a "safe" word that tells them, "Get me out of here!" Then, ask for the check and leave.

**Emotions.** Why do people get so involved or interfere in planning a wedding that isn't even theirs? Why do they have so much to say? Behind all words are emotions. It's my strong belief, after planning weddings for years, that it's a form of grief on their part. Seriously!

People will act their strangest at weddings and funerals. Getting married is not only a major change for your life, it is a change for everyone else close to you. For a parent, this is a milestone event that says life is going by too fast. Your buddies might be wondering if they are losing their friend. Will you have time for them after you are married? A sibling may feel pressure to get married. They may even be asked by others, "When are you getting married? You know it's your turn next!" That can fuel their resentment as they blame you for this new pressure. Reassure them that they are free to ignore the remarks. Remember what it was like to be in their shoes.

Whatever other people feel, don't let them steal your thunder and crush your joy. Their words are only words, not commands. You are the boss of you.

Planning a wedding with your future partner for life is a great exercise for how you will handle life's problems together. Some things you won't agree on, and others you will be in total sync, both in your wedding and in your future. Sometimes you will laugh together, and sometimes you will cry alone. Laughing and crying are both stress relievers. You still love each other.

*Sanity keepers.* I recommend you take one day a week when you don't even utter the "W" word (wedding) to each other. Every time you say the word, put a dollar in a jar. Remember what brought you together in the first place and why you fell in love. Talk about your dreams the way you did prior to the wedding planning! Call it the *Ban "W" Day.* Go on a date, even if only to the bakery to split a cupcake. Taking time out is a good habit to carry into your marriage.

**Memories.** We remember the good times, and weddings are filled with good-time moments. Magic happens as you walk down the aisle. There stands the person you've chosen to spend the rest of your life with, beaming like never before that moment. You never imagined you could feel the way you do as your eyes meet. Your first glance at the reception area, created from your heart and soul, is stunning and rewarding. During the toast, you see someone who never cries, now shedding tears for your happiness. You'll never forget it. Enjoy, remember, and cherish every moment.

# 5

# Matching Priorities with Talent and Pros

# 1

## When DIY (Do It Yourself)
## Turns into DYI (Do Yourself In)

Do-it-yourself (DIY) projects are necessary when your budget is limited. If you enjoy doing crafts, it can be fun and create a happy memory. But don't let it turn from DIY to DYI.

The DIY phenomena is nothing new, but it has grown exponentially with so many online platforms that are a feast for the eyes. For my business alone, I research nearly a hundred different boards on Pinterest. I need to know what people in real life are doing for their weddings. It is one of the best ways to observe current trends. It's a great way to tune in to what people like or to demonstrate an idea to clients. Some sources call something a "trend" in an effort to sell their idea or product, when it doesn't actually reflect what people are doing or wanting. Many of those "trends" are simply not within a couple's budget. If a trend doesn't match my client's vision, I don't push it.

DIY can be fun. DYI happens when you get sidetracked, you buy things just in case, or you don't have time to complete your DIY project. Insufficient time to complete a project causes stress (at best) and wedding delay (at worst). It's heartbreaking when, in spite of your materials, time, work, blood, sweat, and tears, your project doesn't get finished or ends up remaining in a box at the wedding.

Stick to the priorities and themes stated on your Wedding Visionnaire to avoid falling into the DYI trap. If an idea or project aligns with your vision, go for it. If not, skip it. Do you love creating the project? If not, skip it. Don't do it just because you "can," especially if it saps time from other critical elements. If you really want it, it's relaxing to create it, and it fits into your theme, tackle the project and enjoy it!

As a Wedding Planner with strong feelings about the DIY/DYI dilemma,

I offer a complimentary afternoon or evening to help my clients with their DIY projects. It gives me the opportunity to get to know people in the wedding party, to observe family dynamics, and to understand what conflicts a client is facing. And it's good to see the wonderful support of family and friends. It makes a good memory for me and my clients.

Wedding Planners have a variety of skills to help a client through the tough parts of preparation. Because I have a long history of crafting, I can often suggest an easier way to do a project.

### Signs that DIY has morphed into DYI:

1. You bit off more than you can chew and are not getting enough sleep because of rushing to complete a project. (Don't beat yourself up. It happens!)

2. You got in over your head, not having enough knowledge or the proper tools, and you are more frustrated than excited about a project.

3. You said *yes* to one too many suggestions, and you're kicking yourself for not sticking to your guns.

4. You read one too many issues of *Martha Stewart Living*, and your mind is cluttered with ideas.

5. You forgot that you don't have superpowers. Your energy is dwindling or you're feeling anxious. You're human. It's okay to stop, breathe, and reassess.

### The cure:

1. Realize that your time is valuable and the deadline is approaching.

2. Remember that professionals can accomplish things quickly while you tend to other important elements.

3. Before you take on a project, calculate the cost of materials, time, and tools you don't already have. Are you really saving by not hiring a professional?

4. Don't be fooled by thinking that friends or family will help. On the day of your wedding, everybody is out of their element. They are overcome with excitement or nervousness. Seeing a long-lost friend or relative will sidetrack them and make them forget things.

5.  Sometimes a random helper takes over and totally screws up your system and set-up plan. Have a tough, gentle, and reliable leader to help with set up. Without that special person, you risk disaster. Use the KISS method: Keep it super simple!

In the meantime, take stock of all of your crafting supplies and look for bargains on the things you need. Happy crafting to you! I'd love to see some of your projects on Pinterest.

# 2

## Amateurs & Professionals

Assigning tasks to friends or family members can save money. Even when you want to hire a professional, someone in your life may insist on taking photos, baking a cake, cooking your reception dinner, applying makeup, styling hair, arranging your flowers, making chalkboard signs, playing music, or even planning your wedding. Sometimes it works out fine; but quality, reliability, and timeliness often suffer when an amateur takes the helm. "You get what you pay for" holds true when you don't hire a professional. Know what you want and know your priorities. If you rely on friends and family, will you still be on speaking terms after the wedding? It's your wedding!! Don't let anyone talk you into or out of something that makes you uncomfortable.

**The overflowing pool of amateur talent.** It's easy for someone to think that if they have a nice camera, are great at baking cakes, cooking, making flower arrangements, or planning events, they can do it for your wedding. It's done all the time, but often the volunteer is overworked or ill-equipped and unprepared for the magnitude of the task. When Mom is still arranging the buffet while her daughter is walking down the aisle, she misses out on a moment she can never recapture.

*Who are you, and what have you done with my sister?* A wedding day can turn friends and family into people you've never seen before. They're excited and nervous and seeking direction about what they are "supposed to do." Emotions are raw, relationships are on edge, and it can be a setup for the perfect storm. Professionals know these tasks like the back of their hand. Trusting a professional can alleviate stress for you and your family. If you do rely on friends or family, realize that organization, communication, and coordination with them and among them is critical. Thank them profusely; give them the tasks they love; thank them again!

*Aunt Helene is a great cook.* It's one thing to prepare food for ten or twelve people. It's another thing entirely to prepare for fifteen times that number. Different foods require different temperatures to be safe. Not knowing the regulations can not only cause stress but risk illness. Will Aunt Helene cover the expense of chafing dishes and canned heat, serving utensils, and backup equipment? Will there be enough equipment for a double-sided buffet line so that guests can be served twice as fast? Does she know when to discard food to prevent food poisoning? Does she know what is safe to repackage and send home with guests? Will she think ahead of time to prepare plates to keep refrigerated for the newlyweds to eat in their hotel room after the wedding?

*Uncle Bob's fancy camera.* An amateur photographer may have no clue or have even discussed with a couple what shots they want. That's an important and customized discussion! Will the photographer be in sync with the friend playing music so you don't miss out on big moments like the father-daughter dance? Is Uncle Bob aware that editing (if he even does it) takes three or four times as long as it does to actually shoot the photos? Is he prepared in the case of equipment failure? You might not notice anything amiss until you get your pictures—usually much later than you will from a professional photographer—and then realize that someone is missing from a family photo or the photographer didn't capture your first kiss as a married couple.

*Best friend Felicia, flower arranger.* Hours of sleep can be lost the night before the wedding as you and friends make bouquets, boutonnieres, or centerpieces. It is one of the biggest "it's harder than it looks" projects you will encounter. Does Felicia realize the importance of greenery in a bouquet and how much more expensive it can be than the flowers? By the time you realize making your own flower arrangements was not your best decision, it's too late.

A professional florist will be aware of other community events that may cause a shortage of a particular flower or color. Homecomings, proms, and

Mom's Days at universities are just a few non-holiday examples that can affect supply. To do your own flowers, be sure to have several pairs of good gardening gloves and shears to share, plenty of floral tape (stretch it first!), and a first aid kit. Floral designers use special tools to strip the thorns from rose stems. And the greenery that comes in a grocery store flower bundle won't necessarily look good in a bridal bouquet. It may actually stick out like a sore thumb.

*Cousin Jason, wannabe DJ and entertainer.* A DJ is the most important vendor at a wedding reception. Period. End of sentence! The scariest of all amateur substitutes is that cousin who assumes all a DJ needs to do is load up the iPod. My stomach turns to knots when I work a day-of coordination and I don't know the substitute DJ. In contrast, when I do full planning, I help clients choose their vendors. Sometimes amateur substitutes know nothing about weddings. A DJ does a million more things than just play music. I don't usually beg, but please hire a good professional DJ.

*Aunt Beth, the baker.* Is Aunt Beth comfortable making a multi-tiered cake and transporting it so that it stays in one piece or each piece is adequately protected and ready to set up? If she thinks flowers will look nice on your cake, does she know which ones are poison? Is there a proper place to store the cake until the reception, protected from heat, rain, bees, flies, and so forth? Can Aunt Beth design the cake to prevent it from listing or falling over?

*Bob, Jr., videographer.* Uncle Bob's son shoots videos of everything, so he's perfect to shoot for your wedding, right? Find out by asking him how easy it is to edit a three- or four-hour event. Ask if he is discreet about filming people who are beyond drunk or not in their proudest moment. Will he be in people's faces with the camera? Does he think his role is more important than the photographer's? Has he coordinated with the photographer so they won't ruin each other's shots?

**Professional wedding vendors: the unheard voice.** As I wrote this book, I consulted with a number of wedding vendors to help couples understand what vendors do and what couples are purchasing. The media sometimes paints wedding vendors as greedy scammers. I don't respect anyone who tries to scam wedding couples—or anyone, for that matter. But couples need to know the truth. Reputable wedding vendors have a "do not recommend list," which you will do well to heed.

Wedding vendors are artists, creative types with infinite ideas and zest for helping people. These hospitality/helping professionals have one of the highest turnover rates of any similar profession! See it from their side. Vendors who are self-employed may have little profit after their major investments in equipment, networking, advertising, continuing education, and insurance. Many of them only have a few months out of the year to make the money to deliver a good product for their clients. The costs to participate in a wedding show or to advertise on a wedding lead site are astonishing. There are lots of good vendors who don't advertise on these sites, and you need to know how to find them.

A couple who doesn't communicate clearly with their vendors fosters frustration and disaster. Your vendor can't read your mind! Respond promptly to requests for information, and let them know when you've made a change. Even officiants have found themselves at the wrong venue because they weren't informed of a venue change.

Appreciate the value of your vendors' work, and let them know it. It may seem like the vendor's job is fun, not like a real job, but not if you look behind the scenes. As a couple, you might be looking for discounts or even free services, but vendors could easily discount themselves right out of business. The people who ask for discounts and then voice unmerited complaints make vendors question whether it's worth it to grant the discount.

Wedding vendors get more than their share of Monday morning quarterbacking from people who had plenty to drink or only saw a tip of the presentation iceberg. The amateurs don't see disasters that are averted. From my experience, vendors deserve more credit than they get. Maybe there should be a National Wedding Vendor Day.

The media throws the industry under the bus, because that is what sells. Shows are broadcast that portray weddings miles beyond the average budget. Unless a couple is rolling in dough, they need to set priorities, realistic ambitions, and boundaries. Focus on the occasion: marriage to the person you want to spend the rest of your life with. Everything else is just window dressing.

**The wedding vendor as guest.** I attended a wedding as a guest, and I immediately identified the awesome venue coordinator. He had eagle eyes on everything, even before people sat for the ceremony. I liked that he didn't hide from view, like some venue coordinators do.

Excited to meet a fellow wedding professional, I approached him and told him I was a Wedding Planner. He said, "Oh no!" and I immediately backpedaled. "No, no, no!" I said. "I don't mean it like that!" I didn't want him to think I was sizing up everything. He said, "That's not it at all. I always tell my friends not to invite me to their weddings!" I laughed, and the tension broke.

He had a good point. At the end of the event, I told him that I couldn't help but watch him at work. It was poetry in motion. Most people probably didn't see the wedding as I did. I enjoyed eating and dancing. I appreciated the people working the wedding.

A professional's experience at a wedding is almost like a day at the job, whether or not they play a professional role. When I attend weddings that don't employ professionals, I see impending disasters that no one else notices. It's a tough position for me. I try my best to not react to cringe-worthy experiences, but please forgive me if I grimace for no apparent reason. And when I give a sigh of relief, you can too! Just don't expect me to comment about such a wedding from a professional viewpoint. I am happy to point out the good. The rest is none of my business.

PLANNING STAGE

# 6

## Wedding Vendors 101

# 1

# Vendors and Guests

Hiring the right vendors is critical to the overall experience of your wedding day, especially for the reception. A camera does not make a photographer. A bottle opener does not make a bartender. A microphone does not make a DJ. A friend who has helped plan your wedding does not make a Wedding Planner.

**Photographers.** A photographer experienced with weddings has different skills than a family portrait photographer. If they miss the all-important wedding kiss, it's gone forever. I have known photographers who weren't able to get into position to capture that kiss. Some are contortionists and make me hold my breath when they climb to get a good shot. But falling, breaking bones, or ending up in a lake are not good options. A professional recovers by setting up a shot again to capture the essence of the missed moment. Good wedding photographers have much to think about at one time. While anticipating what will happen next, they still manage to capture an image that is unexpected and priceless. It's an art and a science, all at the same time.

Discourteous guests hinder the photographer by stepping up to take a shot, throwing the photographer off balance or into a fall. Guests jump from their seats and raise their phones or tablets into the air, blocking the photographer's line of sight. Backsides, flabby arms, and pop-up bald spots have ruined many a shot. Amateur camera activity from a multitude of devices can also interfere with the sound system or amplify the sound of the photographer's camera. This is a good reason for whomever is conducting the ceremony, to request that all cameras, cell phones, and electronic devices be turned off for an "unplugged ceremony." This protects the professionally documented memories that could otherwise fade and leave future generations missing a priceless connection to previous generations.

**DJs.** I believe DJs are the most important vendor at a reception. They are the eyes, ears, voice, rhythm, and timing. They have to tune in to the crowd and know every working part of the reception. They think in three-minute intervals. They don't just play music—they carefully select each set in collaboration with their clients. With the exception of preparation and photos before the wedding, they implement the major timeline for the wedding day. They diligently set up and test sound and lighting equipment.

DJs and Wedding Planners are usually the first to arrive and the last to leave. If there is no Wedding Planner, the DJ must work in conjunction with other vendors to make a timeline for the reception to flow. They prepare for the special surprise moments a couple has in store. DJs have the less glamorous (but important) task of announcing that someone left their car lights on, a car is being towed, or a neighbor is complaining about a barking dog in a car. They announce lost-and-found items and reconnect stray toddlers with their parents. The DJ and the Wedding Planner are the grease that makes everything run like a finely tuned machine.

**Bartenders.** Some people are good bartenders. Other people serve drinks. Like the DJ, a bartender's responsibility goes beyond serving drinks. They are responsible to not over-serve anyone or to serve anyone underage. They expertly calculate how much alcohol and what types to serve. Bartenders may differ from each other in the amount and kind of insurance and licenses they carry.

**Wedding Planners.** Wedding Planners have many roles. At the reception, we aim to spot problems before they arise so that you can enjoy your wedding day oblivious to potential or prevented disasters. Planners are the liaison for vendors, clients, and guests, so that clients are properly informed and can leave their worries behind. We also read the crowd to tend to people with special needs due to age or physical condition. When we see someone alone or uncomfortable in the crowd, we may strike up a casual conversation to put a smile on their face.

**Guests.** Guests can be difficult for vendors and embarrassing for the bride and groom. I've seen it mushroom to the point of physical assault on the poor vendors. As a couple, be responsible for the type of day you want to remember. Consider informing guests of the kind of behavior you expect or forbid. Think seriously about your guest list and trust your gut. The respect for venue rules is disappearing to the point that one popular venue in my area was converted to an assisted living facility!

Do you need to establish a "dress code" for behavior or offer "pre-flight" instructions? *May I have your attention, please? If an unruly passenger (guest) poses a danger to the crew (vendors) or passengers (guests), we will land at the next available airport (stop the wedding reception) with law enforcement officers (security or police) waiting. Belligerence toward any of the flight attendants (vendors) or refusal to comply with airline (venue) rules, will be rewarded with the task of cleaning the restrooms.*

Police and security should never have to play a major role at a wedding.

# 2

# Overtaxing
# the Vendors

You hire a vendor for a specific job. Don't saddle them with duties and details that aren't part of their job description or skill set. It takes them out of their own lane of responsibility. A photographer should not have to help with the ceremony setup in order to get the shots they need. A caterer should not have to line up the wedding party to start the processional. A DJ should not have to help set up tables just because he or she is one of the first vendors at the venue. An officiant should not be setting up chairs or pinning on boutonnieres. A floral designer should not have to set up the cake table just because they have flowers to be placed on the cake. A pastry chef shouldn't have to search for utensils needed to serve the cake.

Wedding vendor burnout is real! When each vendor can concentrate on their specific job, everything runs smoothly. Don't take undue advantage. Wedding vendors are people, too. Let them do what they are hired to do. Supply and demand for wedding vendors influences prices. Don't burn them out and drive them from the industry.

# 3

# Don't Set Yourself Up
# for Regret

The most common time that couples or their families wish that they had hired a Wedding Planner or a Videographer is just before or just after a wedding. That's when it becomes apparent how much work was involved, how some people missed special moments because they were "working" instead of just enjoying the wedding.

**Wedding Planner.** In a family with two daughters, the second daughter is likely to engage a Wedding Planner if the first daughter did not. Witnessing a disaster at someone else's wedding is incentive to hire a Wedding Planner for your own. Some Wedding Planners can take on a wedding four to eight weeks prior to the event, but it's not preferred, because by then there are loose ends and mistakes to be corrected. A "Wedding Planner" without a business license is likely not a professional and won't take it as seriously as a licensed professional.

**Videographer.** Regret for missed moments during the wedding day sets in after the fact. Our dear friends and loved ones eventually pass away. It is comforting to look back at quality videos and see a loved one's mannerisms, hear their voice, and remember their better days. People call their videographer years later to thank them again for the video. A videographer creates future comfort. A video captures lasting memories that engage the senses of hearing and sight. Some vendors offer both photography and videography service. Photography is good, but a quality recording adds another dimension to captured moments.

# 4

# Feeding
# the Vendors

**Communicate with your caterer.** Accounting for guests and the wedding party is such a big task that couples often don't even think about feeding the vendors. Remember that vendors and their assistants are pretty much "grounded" for the wedding day. They need sustenance! Some vendors will write into their contracts that they will be fed.

Discuss with your caterer how best to feed your vendors. Caterers will have a variety of options. If your budget won't cover the same fare for your vendors as for guests, the caterers can prepare a less expensive version. If they suggest a boxed meal, be aware of any potential food sensitivities or allergies. It may be easier to give them the same entree choices as your guests or let them go through the buffet line. Some caterers automatically include vendors when they plan how much food to prepare. Let your caterer know who and how many vendors and assistants will be working through the wedding day. Alcohol should NOT be provided for vendors.

**Walk in your vendors' shoes.** Vendors work more hours for a wedding than you will ever see. In addition to service, they have equipment (some of which is heavy and sensitive), supplies, or food to deliver and unload and then load again to return. They have travel time. They spend hours on their feet. Vendors are often the first to show up on the wedding day and among the last to leave. They need food to sustain the energy to perform their tasks throughout your entire wedding day. This applies to your Wedding Planner, videographer, photographers and their second shooters, the DJ, and any other vendors who are there for the duration of the wedding reception.

**Feeding time.** It's a palm-to-forehead moment when you realize that vendors need to eat *when everyone else is eating*. People don't like to be photographed while they are eating, so let the photographers go through the buffet line right after the family and bridal party. That way they will be ready to shoot the cake cutting, toasts, and important dances. Let the remaining vendors eat just before the last of the tables are called to the buffet. They need enough time and a place to eat, whether at a vendors' table in another room or in empty seats at one of the guest tables. Vendors may prefer not to eat with the guests, because they need to eat quickly and get back to their tasks. Photographers need enough time to eat but not miss any shots. Hold the toasts, the cake cutting, and the first dance until the vendors are done eating. Let the DJ eat when there's background music during the dinner.

# 5

## Other Vendors

You might be asking, "How do I find somebody that does XYZ, and how do I know they are reputable and qualified? Wedding Planners have a lot of sources for just about any vendor category.

**Setup and cleanup.** People sometimes assume that friends and family will hang around to help clean up after a reception. Sorry to break it to you, but for tearing down (even more so than setting up) this seldom happens the way you think it will. You definitely won't want to hang around to supervise this at your wedding. Think how much work it is just to clean up after a small party. For a wedding, you can't postpone cleanup until the next day. As tired or as inebriated as people might be, cleanup must happen, or you risk forfeiting your deposit or incurring additional rental hours. Each venue is different, but don't expect much leeway.

Many housecleaning or commercial cleaning companies will jump at the chance do post-wedding cleanup. Consult with them and be prepared with venue rules, rental company rules, what to toss and what to keep, etc. Some companies specialize in setting up weddings and then returning to tear down afterwards. Communication with your venue and any other vendors who will be picking up items after the wedding is key.

**Childcare.** Whether your guests have children or not, they will thank you for provisions for onsite childcare. Use a babysitting service or inquire at a community college in the childcare or education programs to see who might like some hours towards a class requirement. Make sure that everyone is properly insured and accredited.

Why would I recommend a childcare service over a couple of teenage friends? Teenage friends will be more interested in what is going on during the reception than in staying in a room with little kids. You want someone who will give full attention to the children—someone who won't be distracted by texting, surfing the internet, or chatting on the phone. Consider setting up age-appropriate activities for your tiniest guests. Safety is the first concern. Go with the pros if you can, and educate yourself on the services they provide.

**Pet sitter.** It's surprising how many people forget until the last minute to find a sitter for Fido or Fifi for the wedding day and for the honeymoon. Finding a pet sitter can be challenging if it's not planned for in advance. You might need extra time for your animals and the caregiver to get acquainted. Some people have their fur babies participate in the wedding. A professional pet sitter can bring the dog to the wedding long enough to perform the duties of flower dog or ring bearer dog, pose for a few pictures, and then take the dog home.

**Coat-check services.** Coat-check services do exist, but some of your other vendors may offer this as an additional service. Ask if your limo vendor or an event staffing company or even your venue offer this service. It requires a constant eye on the items that are being checked. They can also attach cards to unmarked gifts so that you know who all the givers are. Your guests may appreciate this service more than any favors you would provide. Your guests spent, time, money, and effort to purchase a gift just for you. Guests will truly enjoy your day when they don't have to worry about their items or gifts being stolen. And your pictures will look better without coats hanging on the backs of chairs.

**Ice-cream cart.** I want to share one of my biggest wedding planning "aha!" moments. It seems the majority of men in our society do not typically enjoy going to weddings. Well, as the saying goes, "The way to a man's heart is through his stomach." My eyes were opened wide the first time a client acted on my recommendation to hire an ice-cream cart. I had no idea how well-loved that cart would be! Grown men of all ages were NOT sitting in their seats or checking their watches to see how much longer they had to endure. They all but blazed a trail through the grass to the cart! I overheard men saying, "I tried that flavor, now I'm going to try the other flavors," and, "That flavor was good in a dish, now I want to try it in a cone!" These men were definitely not bored. The math for how many variations they would create was incalculable. The ice-cream cart trick will turn men from party-poopers into contented participants. Get approval from your venue. For added RSVP ammo, consider announcing on your invitations that there will be an ice-cream cart at the reception. Be sure to hire the cart before you send out invitations so you don't risk disappointment if the cart's not available.

**Weddings on steroids.** Gone are the days when it was common and acceptable for a wedding to consist of the ceremony followed by a reception with cake, nuts, and beverages, with music and dancing optional. Now, the trend is to provide entertainment or activities in addition to a DJ. Some activities become a substitute for party favors. Consider these vendors to add extra memories to your wedding day. They might even be the highlight of the reception that makes your wedding unique.

- Coat check service
- Caricature artist
- Magician
- Photo booth
- Ice-cream cart
- Dessert truck
- Food truck
- S'mores dessert station
- Horse-drawn carriage
- Electronic graffiti wall

Whatever you imagine, you can produce! Check out <u>animatemyevent.com</u> for fun, exciting, entertaining ways to serve beverages and cake.

Choose the vendors that resonate with you to "brand" your wedding, to weave your personalities, and make your story come to life. Your wedding day will go more smoothly and provide you and your guests with happy, unique memories.

# 7

## Study, Spy, and Then Say Hi

**Vendor consultations.** Before you consult with a vendor, make sure they have a business license. A business license tells you they take their role seriously. For your sake and for the sake of the vendor, do your homework. It doesn't take much, but you want to avoid assumptions and go into a consultation with an open and informed mind.

Showing up on time for your consultation gets you off to a good start. Don't start a consultation by asking, "How much do you charge?" And shy away from a vendor who opens with, "What is your budget?" Granted, those are easy ice-breakers, but I propose a different approach.

Check out vendors' websites, Facebook business page portfolios, Instagram, Pinterest, or other platforms. A blog will give you a feeling for their personality, almost like having a conversation. This is particularly true for Photographers, and you really get to know the style from viewing their work. No two vendors are alike. Sometimes you will find a vendor whose style immediately appeals to you. Check them out at shows as well as online.

Wedding vendors are creative, not just in their artwork but also with their ideas and solutions. They bring their personality into their work. As a Wedding Planner, I try to have the perfect vendor/client combination in mind after my initial client consultation. Sometimes I can easily select sixteen vendor categories within six to eight weeks. It's like introducing the client and the vendor to a new friend.

It takes a lot of time for a Wedding Planner to develop those relationships and match a client's needs and desires. For instance, if a photographer doesn't make you smile or makes you uncomfortable in your consultation, think twice about hiring them. That's one reason photographers do complimentary engagement photo sessions with a couple. Both parties will know if it isn't a match. They like to get to know you before your wedding to do their best work on your wedding day. Even if you don't hire them for the event, you can still purchase the photos from the engagement session. If you do hire them, your engagement session fee may be applied to your final photography package. I wouldn't match a quiet, shy client with a domineering personality, and I wouldn't pair an aggressive client with a timid vendor. There's a happy medium that works to create the best partnership.

This book tells you what you should know about each vendor category before you begin your consultations. I tell you what to expect, suggest questions to ask, and give you insight about why a vendor charges "so much"! I relay things every vendor wishes you knew before a consultation.

Wedding vendors need to make a living. They work hard, and they are natural helpers. They love what they do, but they have bills to pay: advertising costs, training, wedding shows and open houses, and hours of costly networking.

I recommend you consider hiring professional vendors in the categories that are most important to you. Some things you don't want to leave to chance. Criticism or "I-can-do-that-ism" comes easier than craftsmanship. The pros make things look easy. For the do-it-yourselfer, it's not as easy as it seems to nail the look we admire in a vendor's work. Learn about vendors you might not even think you need. They could end up being the ones who give you the most relief.

Time is money. But remember, the more you opt to do it yourself, the busier you will be the week before the wedding. A lot happens during the month prior to the wedding, and that last week can be a killer! You might want to have a Wedding Planner who has a month-of or day-of coordination plan. A day-of coordinator does more work before the wedding than on the actual wedding day. You'll see more about this in the next Planning Stage.

Enjoy and your consultations with vendors. No one works harder to help create a wedding that has your name written all over it.

# 8

## Your Event Producer/Director:
## The Wedding Planner

**Avoid wedding day regrets.** Wedding Planners are among the vendors that people most regret not hiring. Regret sets in just before the wedding, when the couple suddenly realizes the vast amount of work to be done in a short amount of time. Regret also sets in right after the wedding, when tensions run high with friends or family who feel like they have been overworked and underappreciated.

**Misconceptions.** A faulty assumption is that Wedding Planners costs too much. In fact, they often can save you as much or more than the fee by preventing mistakes, knowing the work of vendors, offering extensive resources, and focusing on your priorities. Vendors appreciate Wedding Planners as a source of complimentary marketing and a reassurance of less stress for the event. Vendors often pass a discount to clients who have hired a professional Wedding Planner. The reduction of stress alone is priceless. Don't be surprised if one of the first questions a vendor asks is if you have hired a Wedding Planner. Your guests will appreciate the organization and flow that a Wedding Planner provides.

**Experienced parents.** Parents who understand the stress of wedding planning can fund the Wedding Planner as a gift for their son or daughter. It is an act of love and a gift to themselves. I've heard mothers say the only thing they want to do is buy a dress and sit down at the wedding. Hiring a Wedding Planner allows that to happen.

**The nitty-gritty truth.** As with any wedding vendor, you see only the tip of the Wedding Planner iceberg on the wedding day. When people tell me it would be fun to be a Wedding Planner, I tell them the truth. First, it's not glamorous. Second, get two pairs of *comfortable* shoes to wear at each event; otherwise your feet will hurt like hell! On the big day, it is not uncommon to spend sixteen hours running hither and yon, inside or outside over ten acres of land. If it takes only one day to recover from a wedding, you're in good shape. If it takes two days, you're doing pretty well. Three days, maybe you should rethink it. Four days? Retire!

**Advisor only.** Are you worried that a Wedding Planner will take over your wedding? A good Wedding Planner will never do that. An experienced Wedding Planner will make your wishes top priority. Sometimes we have to remind *other* people (dare I say, mothers?) of what you want. This only works if you are completely honest and have constant dialogue with your Wedding Planner. It's your job as the couple to communicate any changes you want and to be decisive under the guidance of your Wedding Planner.

**Professional experience.** Experienced Wedding Planners know the wedding industry as a whole, better than any other type of wedding vendor. We can sense your uncertainty and inspire you with new ideas. We know when something you want will not work without more details and attention. While we want to bring your vision to life, we will let you know if one of your intended elements might go over like a lead balloon. If it's not illegal, life-threatening, or unethical, we will try to make it happen! We will suggest ways to create the same ambience or accomplish the same purpose in a way that you can kill two birds with one stone. We love saving money for our clients by helping them make frugal decisions that make them happy in the end.

Couples assume a lot of things that can result in unnecessary costs. It's not your fault! You only know what you know. A good Wedding Planner will know if something you want is thought out well enough to be successful. A good Wedding Planner will never try to force you to adopt the latest trends. Know and communicate your priorities. If something is unrealistic for your budget, a good Wedding Planner will tell you that.

**Relax, enjoy, create memories.** My Wedding Planner motto is: *It's not the best seat in the house if you're not in it!* If you, your friends, or your family are tending to details during the wedding or reception, you will miss the once-in-a-lifetime moments! You should also be enjoying precious moments with your family and friends during the month before the wedding.

Most Wedding Planners will have everything coordinated at least a month prior to the event, leaving only the final guest count to report to the caterer, officiant, venue, and the rental companies. When my clients cooperate, I can complete the major planning and have all vendor contracts signed within two months. I've even accomplished this for couples who gave me only six months to plan an entire August wedding—the busiest wedding month in their region.

**A surprise about Wedding Planners.** Nearly every year, event planners rank in the top five for most stressful job, right along with police officers, firefighters, airline pilots, and enlisted military personnel. In the worst of circumstances, we encounter those other professionals at weddings or other events. We so appreciate those men in uniform—we would just rather not have to meet them in their line of duty at a wedding. The only uniforms we want to see at a wedding are dress blues on the groom or groomsman.

**Planning packages.** Wedding Planners offer a variety of options ranging from **à la carte services** to full planning and everything in between. Even when you are half-way through your planning, it's not too late to find a Wedding Planner who can ease your burden with whatever is left to plan. Remember that most weddings take place within a few months in any given region, so you might have competition. Act on your search sooner than later to ensure availability. Consider that travel fees may be added for weddings that are beyond the normal service area of a Planner. Lodging may be required if they have to be at a rehearsal the evening before or if the wedding reception runs late into the evening.

Check prospective Wedding Planners' websites to see what packages they offer. Let's cover the broader details, then we'll dive deep into the subject of a day-of coordinator—the most common package that Wedding Planners are hired to do. Here are some common planning packages:

> *Full Planning.* A full planning option is one that usually includes a Wedding Planner sourcing your vendors "3-deep" (with at least three vendors per category) and managing the wedding day. The Wedding Planner would accompany you on most, if not all, vendor consultations. They would develop a wedding-day timeline and review all contracts so that they match your vision. They can be the liaison on your behalf if you need an explanation from a vendor or need to pass information to a vendor. They can accept deliveries on your behalf or oversee setups for rentals. They will

be at your wedding hours before and hours afterwards. Sometimes their contract includes a set number of hours, after which they will charge more.

*Deluxe Planning.* A deluxe planning package is very customized and more expensive, but people love them. Sometimes they include a full planning option with a lot of à la carte extras. I love to plan these! A deluxe item might be to use the RSVP tracking services or the option to prepare welcome baskets for out-of-town guests upon arriving at their hotel. Deluxe planning can include a huge variety of options.

*Day-of Plus.* A perfect planning option if you've found a few vendors and still need more, but you simply don't have the time and energy for it, is like a day-of coordination on steroids. It's commonly known as a "day-of plus." It works when you want someone to manage the wedding and reception, but you also need help getting just a few more vendors.

All of these planning packages should include a timeline of the wedding day to be shared with each and every vendor and will also include the contact information and arrival time of those making deliveries. The Wedding Planner again will review the vendor contracts to see if your vision matches what's in the contract. This is just the tip of the iceberg of what a Wedding Planner will do for you. While most Wedding Planners provide many of the same services, they also do things to set themselves apart from others and add a twist to the way they plan weddings.

No matter what planning option you choose, your professional Wedding Planner will likely bring an emergency kit for your wedding day. The one I provide is stocked with items from these shopping aisles: travel samples, back-to-school, first aid, tummy ache, feminine hygiene, makeup/makeup remover, hair care, pantyhose, sewing, and cleaning products. I pack it all into an under-the-bed shoe storage container on wheels and include an inventory list with instructions to either "throw away," "put this in the pouch to be sanitized," or "keep it." It's an impressive enough assembly that one photographer actually took a picture of it. Typically, the most requested items were the sewing kit, the blister patches, and Tylenol.

*Day-of Coordination: the Deep Dive.* I promised you a deep dive into the most popular planning option: day-of coordination. Let me stress the point that day-of coordination is NOT about just one day. A real Wedding Planner does not just show up at a wedding and expect to manage it. It's hard to believe that a day-of coordinator (DOC) can put in as much as forty hours of work prior to the wedding. That forty hours of work could include contacting all vendors/amateurs with roles, reviewing contracts to see that they match your vision, creating a timeline, and possibly a rehearsal. But some Wedding Planners will tell you that being a DOC is more difficult than full planning. That is true when the DOC has to work a wedding with lesser experienced vendors or people like friends or family who don't know the big picture of the wedding day.

Some Wedding Planners won't offer DOC packages, even though it is the most common planning requested. While it is less expensive than full planning, it has other drawbacks. The horror stories we could tell would come off sounding like fiction! Your Wedding Planner wants nothing more than for an event to go smoothly, and DOCs definitely facilitate that.

Do some research online *in addition* to the big websites that claim to be the hub of everything wedding. Vendors pay dearly to be on those sites, and sometimes we feel ignored in their process. The big companies tend to forget the hands that feed them, and they may claim that their platform is capable of planning an entire wedding. The difference between the all-inclusive companies and a Wedding Planner are that for us it's personal, but for them it can be just a transaction. Major faux pas when a vendor claims—right in front of us—that they can plan our client's entire wedding. Did they forget who brought them the client? Those vendors or websites won't attend consultations for sixteen to twenty sub-vendors (times three), nor will they be the first one at the site and the last to leave.

**Super powers and mythical creatures.** Good Wedding Planners will turn on a dime to avert disasters before they happen. They take care of things that you won't even be aware of. Our goal is to minimize the effect of Murphy's Law. Wedding Planners are *your* advocate throughout the planning process. We fend off friends or family who try to block what you want.

For a mother who is planning a wedding on behalf of her daughter, I ask, "what does SHE want?" If you don't want to toss your bouquet, we will see that you aren't forced into it by a drunk relative or guest. If you don't want your attendants to wear the same color of dress, we will quietly take the fashionista aside and explain that it is your wedding, and it will be beautiful.

We sometimes gently tell a mother that her little girl is growing up, encourage her to be proud of that independence and celebrate her dream wedding, even if it's different from what Mom imagined. This is not a slight against Moms, but an important show of mutual respect and gratitude. Purse strings should not be used as puppet strings, nor should those parents who are paying for the wedding be ignored or taken for granted.

As much as everyone wants perfection, beware of the little wedding gremlin looking over your shoulder with a curveball to throw into the mix. Mother Nature, a building, a parking lot, a car tire, a reckless driver, and people with bad attitudes don't take a break just because you're getting married.

How you handle wedding planning and the wedding day itself is a great exercise in how you will handle life as a whole. People will feed off your emotions on your wedding day. The more you roll with the punches, the more relaxed your guests will be. Go with the flow. Laugh at yourselves. Laugh at the things that go haywire. Try not to lose your cool.

Most of all, be nice to each other. When the couple argues or when guests argue, it sets everyone on edge. A wedding is not the place to make enemies or fuel a family feud. Instead, let it be a place to mend family relationships. When that happens, everybody wins!

**Practicality.** Countless wedding vendors have told me that they always encourage their clients to hire a Wedding Planner. It helps the vendors focus on their own tasks and collaborate with other vendors before and during the wedding. The Wedding Planner is available and attentive when the couple doesn't have time to answer. A good planner has all of the details to answer vendor questions.

PLANNING STAGE

# 9

## Let Them Eat Cake—and More

# 1

# Caterers

If at all possible, choose the caterer as soon as you choose your venue (if the venue doesn't provide catering). Venues and caterers prefer you do that about a year in advance. If your wedding is in the off season, you might not need that much notice, but act as quickly as you can to avoid loose ends as the big day approaches.

Caterers are bound by business laws, permitting, and safety regulations. There are onsite and offsite caterers and sometimes they are both. An on-site caterer is housed within a venue such as a hotel or a restaurant with an event space. Catering often helps a restaurant stay in business in a bad economy. Offsite caterers prepare meals on their own turf and deliver to the non-food-service venue, such as a church, that solely provides event space. Such venues might have a kitchen where the caterer can set up or keep food chilled, but they are not equipped for full-on food preparation and service.

Catering facilities are larger than most restaurant kitchens, with more elaborate equipment, walk-in coolers, cleaning and preparation areas. They have a fascinating array of decorations and color schemes to accommodate a variety of events, both buffet style and formal seating. Presentation is everything! Some caterers don't own their own catering space, but rent commercial kitchens to prepare food for an event. It isn't cheap to rent or operate a catering kitchen, and a catering company requires a high caliber of chefs. Know and appreciate that your food is being prepared by the best of the best.

**Misconceptions.** Couples sometimes think that the caterer will coordinate the entire event. A Wedding Planner is the only one who can coordinate your entire event. Some catering packages may include rental items, but they can't coordinate an entire event. Caterers, like Wedding Planners, qualify for discounts on rental items. Some have their own inventory, so you don't have to rent. Ask what their package includes. Don't expect your caterer to do more than their intended purpose.

While caterers fall into two basic categories, the food they cook and how they prepare it varies greatly. Many executive chefs are highly skilled in domestic and ethnic cuisine. This is their passion. Don't be afraid to ask for what you want!

Some people think that catering should cost about the same as dining out at a restaurant. They don't think about the variety of people who are hired specifically for your wedding. Before they even show up, caterers will engage employees and staff in offsite meetings to plan your event as a team to design what you want for your wedding.

**Help your caterer.** As with all wedding vendors, communication is the key. Don't put your event in jeopardy. Respond promptly to your caterer. Keep decision changes to a minimum and communicate them quickly. Keep your appointments. Minimize family involvement. Be decisive. Pay on time (don't risk losing your retainer!). Caterers book a year in advance. Not everyone has a year to plan, so check your catering options as early as possible.

Let your caterer know the composition of your guest count: what percentages will be men, women, children under six, six- to twelve-year-old's, seniors. Each group eats in different quantities, and that calculation can help you avoid overspending—or worse, running out of food! Choose options for children that they are likely to eat. Kids can be hesitant to eat food they're not familiar with but be delighted with macaroni and cheese, hamburgers, or hot dogs.

**Try before you buy.** Ask for a tasting from your caterer or pastry chef before you select your final menu or wedding cake. Tastings come in many forms. Some caterers invite all of their potential clients to sample a variety of their food. It might be complimentary, or there could be a cost per person. Sometimes they charge the couple, and sometimes they charge the Wedding Planner. Some place limits on who can attend.

A caterer may invite you to their "kitchen/showroom" to sample what you think you want to serve. If someone other than the couple is paying, they might want to be there to know what they are getting for their money. Respect the caterers. Don't treat their tastings as a carte blanche tour of free meals.

Your hired caterer will document your decisions on a *Banquet and Event Order* (BEO) with an estimate of all the costs. Every detail—food, beverages, linens, decor, and special notes—will be on the BEO. The only thing missing is the final guest count.

**Pricing variations.** Catering prices are a little bit driven by real estate (location, location, location!). Rents fluctuate in price depending on the part of town they are in. Local economic standards can affect the prices. A hotel or a venue that has onsite catering may waive the space rent with placement of a minimum food order. That threshold is called the *Food and Beverage Minimum.*

Just as you can't predict grocery prices for a big holiday dinner a year in advance, the caterer's cost estimate might change as the wedding date nears. But a caterer should be able to give you a very detailed estimate of what to expect. That is why a retainer is required as well as an accurate guest count. Sometimes the count of professional vendors isn't factored into the budget, and you aren't charged for those meals. Confirm if this is your caterer's policy. Expect to pay a retainer and to pay the balance when you submit the final headcount about fourteen days prior to the wedding.

**Tipping.** In many cases, a service fee (basically a tip) is included in the bill, just as restaurants calculate the tip for a large dinner party.

# 2

## Bartending, Alcohol,
## and Wedding Liability Insurance

If I could stress only one thing, this would be it: *Only someone who has consumed NO alcohol can be a designated driver. Just because someone has had less to drink than others doesn't mean they are safe to drive.*

In 2015, 29% of all traffic fatalities were caused by drunk drivers. A significant percentage of those were "designated drivers." Buzzed driving is drunk driving. Like most people in our country, I've had friends or acquaintances killed or severely injured by a drunk driver. My husband and I were in a high-impact collision with a hit-and-run drunk driver. I still can feel the momentum, thinking it would never stop, and wondering if the next jostling motion would break my neck. In some states, the married couple as host is liable for damage or injury by guests who drive drunk.

Legal judgment aside, you don't want to be responsible for causing someone pain, major surgery, years of physical therapy, rehabilitation, or even death. Don't allow your guests to drive impaired. Uber, Lyft, and local taxis are easily accessible options for safety.

**Trust the pros.** Guests who have had too much to drink spell disaster. And it's not fun to have to load the alcohol you didn't use and cart it away, especially after you have had some of it yourself. A bartending service is required by many venues and facilities, if not legally then by policy, and with good reason. They can suggest, if you are the one to supply the alcohol, where to get it most economically. They know about "signature drinks," some of which are not necessarily alcoholic and can save you money. They can design your wedding signature drink in your color scheme.

**What to expect.** Bartenders do more than serve alcohol. They carefully assess how much and which types of alcohol you're serving according to your guest count. They will want to know the start and end time of your ceremony and reception. They need to know when and where those activities are taking place as they may be noisy during setup and they don't want to interfere with the ceremony.

Talk to potential bartenders, check out their reviews, and decide if your personalities match. A good bartending service will show you proof of insurance and service training. Bartenders can accommodate more people at a consultation than other wedding vendors. Be prepared to pay a 50% retainer fee and to pay the balance about two weeks prior to the wedding. They will charge the same credit card for any last-minute additions or changes that happen during the reception.

A bartender will look for signs that a person has had too much to drink and will not over serve, nor will they serve people who are underage. For that reason, there may not be open wine bottles at guest tables. It's too tempting for underaged drinkers and may contribute to overconsumption. Drink tickets are a wild card. People lose them or give them to others.

Some services have technology to help monitor who has had how much to drink. There are wrist bands that can detect when a limit has been reached before switching from open bar to a cash bar (when guests can pay for their own drinks). See, for example, www.getfastbar.com.

People sometimes consume alcohol before a wedding. Bartenders immediately look for slurred speech, glossed-over eyes, staggering, or any combination thereof. The laws vary from state to state. Know the laws for your state before you consider serving alcohol. The bartending service is there to protect you and to help you have fun. Don't let fun turn into disaster. Remember, you are legally liable for damage or injury due to alcohol, and the consequences can be stiff.

**Last call.** The last call—sometimes announced before the bartending service is about to close—is optional. Bartenders can close up at any time if they perceive that no more alcohol should be served. The down side of the last call is that it's usually close to the time when people will be leaving, when they might better focus on sobering up than having more to drink.

**Insurance.** Don't risk the liability of disaster due to alcohol that you provide. Be sure your bartending service is properly insured. *Your venue may also require you to have event insurance, which covers more than just alcohol liability.* If a bartending service has adequate insurance, it could save you a lot of headache.

Check out <u>WedSafe.com</u> or consider getting a rider on your renters' or homeowners' insurance or even AAA auto insurance. Compare the coverage with that of event insurance and decide which product serves you best. Event insurance may cover things like vendor cancellations and venue insurance. Using your homeowners' or renters' insurance may trigger a rate hike if you file a claim. Do your research and choose the plan (or plans) that relieve your stress.

# 3

⋄⋄⋄⋄⋄⋄⋄⋄⋄⋄⋄⋄⋄⋄⋄⋄⋄⋄⋄⋄⋄⋄⋄⋄⋄⋄

# Pastry Chefs
# & Wedding Cakes

The term "pastry chef" reflects extensive training of people who make wedding cakes and other varieties of pastries. Their talents have been developed beyond those who make and decorate cakes.

**Not all cakes are created equal.** Because cake design and decoration is an art—not just in appearance, but in taste, texture, filling, and frosting—meet with at least three cake vendors to experience the differences in their work. Some pastry chefs refuse to use fondant. You might thank them for that if you've had negative experiences with fondant, but not all fondants are created equal. The ingredients can make a difference between "just another wedding cake" and one that has people begging for seconds.

**Your perfect wedding cake.** An experienced Wedding Planner can tell you which pastry chefs stand out from the rest. You may love cake or hate cake. Some people hate frosting, others love it. Some are sensitive to the moisture content of the cake. Frosting varies greatly from one pastry chef to another. Know what you like in a cake, and search for that. You can learn a lot about a pastry chef's ability from their website or social media reviews, but don't just look at the wedding cakes. Check out their other creations like cake pops and mini cakes. Read their reviews and get on their schedule for a private or group tasting where you can meet the pastry chef.

When you speak to a pastry chef, have a vision of what you want but be open-minded, flexible, and trust the artistic talents and technical knowledge of the pastry chef. With clear communication, expect to be pleasantly surprised.

**Tastings.** We've talked about tastings for the general caterer. There's no substitute for tasting a variety of cakes and experiencing the different types of filling and frosting combinations. It's fun to visit wedding shows and open houses to try samples. I still remember how great my wedding cake tasted years ago, and I've been comparing it to other cakes ever since. Pastry chefs also invite you to sample a variety of cake flavors, fillings, and frostings. How they conduct these tastings varies. They may open their shop to a large number of people for a one-time tasting. They may post their tasting schedules on their website so you can select the date and time that work for you. Wedding show vendors will send you information after the show. Vendors who don't have their own shop might arrange to meet you at a coffee shop or independent business where they will bring samples and allot a specific segment of time for each couple to taste. Some pastry chefs will participate in open houses hosted by venues or catering companies. Open houses provide an intimate setting to talk to vendors.

Enjoy your cake tasting! Feel no guilt. At that moment, it's your job to eat cake!

**What your pastry chef needs to know.** The chef will want to know the color theme for your wedding. Bring swatches and printed copies of ideas (not email attachments) for the pastry chef to keep when you have your first consultation or a tasting appointment. Include design elements of your wedding dress, floral elements, and anything within your theme that can be inspiration for creating your cake. And don't forget the ever-important guest count.

**Pricing and design.** The number of servings from your cake can depend on its shape—square, round, multi-sided—and the number of servings is the base factor in the pricing and design of a cake. Take into account if a significant number of people won't eat cake because they are diabetic or gluten intolerant.

**Gluten-free options.** Because more and more people are choosing gluten-free diets, you might ask your guests to declare dietary requests on the RS-VPs. The options for gluten-free and other specialty cake recipes is on the rise. If this is a major concern, address it in your pastry chef consultations, as not all of them will offer gluten-free solutions. If that's the case, you can accommodate guests with dietary restrictions by using a different source that provides individual portions of what you need. Clearly label the specialty items and be sure they get to the people who require them. Gluten-free cakes cost more and tend to dry out very quickly. They require a larger amount of ingredients, because their layers are not as tall as layers of a regular cake.

Time is money when it comes to the cost of a cake, and decorating is what takes the most time. The more elaborate the design, the more time it takes and the more it costs. Photos of cakes in magazines or on Pinterest are usually more costly than what the average person wants to spend. Your pastry chef is a pro and can guide you to achieve a design you will like for a price that works.

Expect to pay for the time and talent of your Pastry Chef. He or she will ask about the elements of your wedding and your likes and dislikes. Your vision will spark genius in most designers and can result in a cake that has more meaning to you than anything you find in a magazine. It can be done to fit your budget, with some flexibility. As you worked through the Wedding Visionnaire, you chose what is important to you. If cake didn't make the list, don't suddenly request an elaborate cake and expect to stay within your budget.

**Stairs.** Just as with rental companies, whoever delivers your cake will want to know how many stairs they have to climb. That factor might add to the delivery cost. Wedding cakes, being generally rich in butter to make them moist, are heavy.

**The cake table.** Be sure the table for your wedding cake is level. Use a standard level or download the cell phone app that acts as a level. Remember to bring the cake knife and server set and a dish towel to dampen and wipe off the cake knife. Or use a warm glass of water to dip the knife and wipe it. It's also convenient to have a small plate to set the cake knife on to keep the tablecloth from getting messy. Have a couple of plates, forks, napkins, and maybe your champagne glasses on the cake table, ready for when you cut your first slices of the cake!

**Cake and police—protect and serve!** The *time of day* can affect the condition of your cake. You don't want your cake to become a hot mess. Move up the time for cutting and serving the cake if you think temperature or weather may be a problem. Also, a wedding that starts late can make a big difference for the condition of the cake. Think chilled and stable, but the best bet is to simply not have the cake delivered too early in the day.

Protect the cake so that is safe to eat. Be sure the cake table is ready to receive the cake and that someone experienced in handling and delivering large cakes places it properly. Worst case scenario if the weather doesn't cooperate: *Have fun and celebrate with dessert first!*

**Cupcakes, sheet cakes, and a miniature cutting cake.** Cupcakes can be a convenient way to serve your guests, but don't assume that they will be less expensive. As with a wedding cake, it will depend on their size, ingredients, and decoration. Cupcakes are also an option to distinguish gluten-free from regular cake.

Sheet cakes are less expensive than a tiered cake because they have less decorating area. They are also easier to cut and serve. When most of the cake is served from sheet cakes or cupcakes, it's common to have a smaller, tiered, more elaborately decorated cake for the cutting ceremony. After the reception, it's also easier to handle extra sheet cake than whatever is left of a tiered cake. Keep in mind that the ingredients are the same and a pastry chef still needs to make a profit.

If a non-professional will be cutting the cake, be sure your pastry chef shows you or gives you instructions on how to cut the cake and in what size pieces so you don't risk running out of cake.

**Extra cake and the top tier.** It never hurts to ask your pastry chef if they can provide boxes for leftover cake. You can also check in the cake supplies section of your local craft store. Your Wedding Planner might provide a box for saving the top tier. Some pastry chefs opt to bake a complimentary or low-cost smaller cake for a couple to pick up on their first anniversary. That way they don't have to eat stale cake that has been frozen for a year. However, if stored correctly, a high-quality cake can still taste good a year later. Check out the options.

**Pretty, not poison!** Don't pretend that you know how to decorate a cake with flowers and then be the one who poisons all of your guests. This is a drastic DIY mistake! Please, do not put flowers on or near a cake until you speak with a florist and a cake designer. Plants carry toxins, pesticides, and other chemicals on the petals, leaves, and stems. If you want your cake decorated with flowers, have your florist coordinate with the pastry chef for the look that you want and the types of flowers you want. Go pro or risk going to the ER when you decorate your cake with flowers.

**Transporting the cake.** I would strongly discourage you from picking up the wedding cake rather than having the pastry chef or their team transport and set it up. This is another DIY that saves money but begs for disaster. Not many Wedding Planners advise clients to transport and set up the wedding cake. And most don't want to be responsible for the cake. Please, go with the cake pros for transport.

**Styrofoam cakes.** Why would you want a Styrofoam cake? The display cakes you see in bakeries are made of Styrofoam. Some people don't want to invest in a cake, so they order from a company that makes Styrofoam cakes with a section cut out to hold a box of two slices of cake. If you want to add height to the cake with minimal decoration, Styrofoam can be a design option. If you want a cake for appearance only, you will still pay for the biggest time and cost element for a wedding cake—decorating. Savings are minimal, at best.

PLANNING STAGE

# 10

## Tell Them Where to Go!

# 1

# The Stationer's Expertise

I love the intricacies of the artistic side of wedding vendors, stationers included. People look at printed materials and say, "That looks easy enough. I could do that." That thinking puts couples in trouble with their budgets and creates unwanted frustration with themselves and others. Criticism comes easier than craftsmanship. Think you can simply buy some calligraphy pens and ink and play around to get an appreciation of the skillset? It might be fun, but not so much when you're under the pressure of deadline. Invitations are a great way to express your authenticity. If you're set on crafting your own, find a stationer that offers classes on making invitations.

**Printing.** Why not just print your invitations and other items yourself online? People will throw them out, right? Not so fast! Many people (and they're not all from one generation) are reluctant to set up a Facebook account to RSVP for a wedding. People will more likely keep your wedding date in mind and remember to RSVP if they repeatedly see your invitation posted on the refrigerator.

Have a website or event page if you wish, but know that it won't accommodate every one of your guests. The older generations will cherish a memento of your special day, especially if they are unable to attend. What I'm saying is, don't paint everyone with a broad brush when it comes to invitations.

But wait! So much more is going on in the world of paper than meets the eye.

**Avoiding mistakes.** One reason to hire someone to take care of all the printed items is to avoid making a mistake. Sometimes I've had to remind clients that the number of invitations won't equal the guest count unless every single guest has a separate address. One invitation per married couple or family will suffice. Do send separate invitations for each roommate who shares an address.

Stationers are the experts on protocol and etiquette for some very important details. Are you certain what information needs to be included on the different printed pieces? It's easy to bungle the wording or leave something out. How do you express that children are not welcome? How do you word it so that people won't wear jeans and tee-shirts to your tux-and-tails event? If you say, "dressy casual," what the heck does that mean? Is it the same for everyone? How do you graciously insist people be on time?

Here's a perfect example why a professional stationer is a good idea: https://www.thesun.co.uk/living/1682513/wedding-invite-with-rather-unusual-meal-choice-sends-social-media-into-meltdown/. Your stationer is a wordsmith and artist who can craft the best message for common "sensitive subjects" and eliminate confusion about how to reply.

**What stationers want you to know.** Google is a vast source of conflicting and out-of-date information. Much of what you find is general and not applicable to different cultures or religions. Family units go way beyond Mom, Dad, and kids. How will your wording reflect all possibilities?

Online sources may not take into account all the moving parts. What do your guests need to know before the wedding for an accurate RSVP? What do they need to know when they arrive at the site? Will there be maps, programs, menus, signs, table numbers, seating charts, escort cards, or place cards? And don't forget thank-you notes! Independent stationers will separate themselves from someone taking the DIY route by using quality papers and inks for true colors that won't run. The independent stationer is a one-stop shop to take care all your printing concerns.

**Time and quality.** A professional stationer will save you valuable time, and extra time is a commodity that most couples don't have. What could you be tending to instead of addressing, stuffing, sealing, and stamping envelopes? Writer's cramp can set in when you're writing out escort cards and place cards. There goes one more to the recycling bin when you spell someone's name wrong! And the quality of handwriting goes downhill as you tire out or combine the task with too much wine.

**The invitation.** An invitation is like a front-door welcome mat. It sets the tone, theme, and the anticipation of what is on the other side of the door. Some guests run out and buy an outfit to match the wedding invitation colors. How fun! Bulk invitations lack the personality of custom design. And if the store count is short by a few, you have to buy another whole box. The office supply store won't present the warm welcome you want for your guests.

**From idea to reality.** Printing vendors want to hear your ideas, and they can tell you if your ideas fit your budget. What do you like about different elements of a design? What in particular attracts you to a sample that you like? Be open to your stationer's creative genius, and know that your story will be the real guide to create the final product that you love.

**Reception logistics.** *Escort cards* are essential for a sit-down dinner or buffet. The escort card guides a guest to their table. The *place card* identifies where they will sit at a table. The place card should show in words or with color coding the guest's meal selection. This ensures servers will bring each guest the correct meal. A seating chart will save you money by eliminating the need for extra tables, chairs, linens, and centerpieces. That savings alone could pay for the postage for your invitations.

**Pricing and experience.** If you feel that stationers charge too much, conserve by hiring a stationer only for the parts that you dread most when you consider doing it yourself. Until you understand the cost of equipment and supplies, overhead, and time spent, it's hard to appreciate the price tag for a stationer. This isn't a hobby for them; it puts food on their table. Expect to pay a 50% non-refundable retainer and to pay the balance plus shipping costs before you receive any products.

Design and print takes time, so don't wait until the last minute to hire someone. If you know the date, the venue, the colors and/or theme for your wedding, consult with a stationer so your Save-The-Dates (affectionately known in the wedding industry as "STDs") are sent out in time. Tell them everything: the flowers you hope to have and what you like from the stationer's website, blog, Pinterest, Instagram, or Facebook pages. Refer to your

Wedding Visionnaire form, remember your priorities and your intended budget, and consider the value of *your* time, money, and stress. Remember your dreams and your vision.

Online examples will not necessarily fit your budget, and a good stationer will not steal another artist's work. Give them creative license, but be realistic about the materials and time involved.

# 2

# RSVPs

RSVP is a French abbreviation for *répondez s'il vous plaît*. It means "please respond." While most people know what it means, getting some to actually respond can be harder than teaching them French. The percentage of people who don't RSVP and show up anyway is on the rise. The number of people who do RSVP and then don't show up also seems to be increasing.

Nothing drives a couple crazier than the lack of RSVPs as the wedding approaches. Even people guilty of the same lack of response for other people's weddings change their attitude when it's their turn to beg for RSVPs. Suddenly, the words, "We just thought you knew we would come to the wedding," have a different ring to them. They think, "The groom's my buddy. He'll expect me to bring my girlfriend and my sister and her kids. I'm sure there will be plenty of food."

Some stationers and some Wedding Planners offer RSVP tracking services. I've discovered that the rate and the speed at which RSVPs are received goes up significantly if people have to mail their responses to a business. It's a psychological mystery. While it's true that a lower guest count means lower costs, it doesn't apply when people return an RSVP and then don't show up. Common courtesy—ahhhh, if only it were common. Here's a tip: Write a number on the back of each RSVP card to correspond with your guest list. When people forget to write their names on the RSVP card, you'll be one step ahead! This reminder came from a recent bride who read the original manuscript. Thank you, Elizabeth!

**RSVPs to gauge costs.** RSVPs are a major factor to determine costs for a million things, especially involving the reception. What's *not* affected by RSVPs? They affect the cost of everything the guests are given to hold, to eat, and to sit on during the wedding and the reception. When a table is littered with unclaimed escort cards, the couple cannot recoup the cost of those wasted meals. You can't simply send home extra food with your guests without complying with health codes and equipment requirements.

**RSVPs to gauge food.** Your caterer will want a "preliminary final" head-count about fourteen days before the wedding, with an absolute final head count closer to the wedding date. Better to count too high than too low. The count determines not only food, but glasses, stemware, linens, and flatware, not only for guests but for the number of employees required to work the event.

**RSVPs and venue.** Hopefully, your rented venue will accommodate all of the stationary and moving parts of the wedding. A venue is one of your biggest expenses, and even if a significant number of people are no-shows, you still have to pay for the whole space. It's even worse to be kicked out of a venue because you've gone over the legal capacity for a space. If the fire safety codes are violated, the wedding can or will be shut down. Save-The-Date cards that go out relatively early will decrease the proportion of non-responders when it's time to RSVP.

**Bad apples.** Sometimes you have to think for adults as well as for kids. State pertinent rules on your invitations or provide a link to the venue's rules, if possible. Think long and hard about who might cause a ruckus after having a few drinks. Damage deposits are not inexpensive. Don't shy away from stating your expectations and make them aware of the venue's expectations. You may want to add that the wedding ceremony will be unplugged (for the sake of the photographer, DJ, and officiant). Higher wedding costs are due in part to the behavior of disruptive and destructive guests. Venues and vendors need to protect their investment and the equipment they use week in and week out. When the industry experts gather to discuss how to deal with unruly guests and protect themselves and their property, you know it's a serious problem. Their most viable option is to charge more.

**RSVPs, furniture, and decor.** Furniture includes tables, chairs, dance floor, and any other special touches you add for the ambience you want to create. Fewer guests call for a smaller dance floor and fewer decor details such as non-floral centerpieces, tablecloths and napkins, table runners, over-lays, chair covers, and sashes. A good and timely RSVP count cuts costs.

**Solving the RSVP dilemma.** Here's my solution for a reception with a buffet line—even more crucial for a plated dinner. Set up one more table than the RSVPs require. Put it in the back and don't make it as noticeable as the other tables. Give it a table number, but no centerpiece, chair sashes, or other decor items. Just a table with a tablecloth and chairs.

This unadorned table is for people who don't RSVP but show up anyway and expect to be fed, served beverages, join in the toast, and enjoy cake. Call this "Table Zero," as there won't be escort cards to direct them since they didn't RSVP. The table will probably have a different number on it or called by a name other than Zero, but you get the point. It should be in the least noticeable area of your reception. Hopefully, they won't sit in a seat assigned to someone else. Place cards to the rescue, again!

How do you make this happen without looking like a slime ball while you deal fairly with the situation? Your DJ—arguably the most crucial vendor at a wedding reception—can work in conjunction with the caterer, bartenders, and whoever cuts the cake to release the tables in a variety of ways with Table Zero being the last to go through the buffet line, the last to be served drinks (especially for toasting), and the last to receive cake. Most caterers do prepare for slightly more than the number of your guest count, but not enough to count on feeding every extra person who shows up without having responded to you.

The guests who RSVP deserve the best environment and the best seats in the house. They should not have to scrape the bottom of the chafing dishes in the buffet line or miss out on cake or the wedding toast. Table Zero addresses the problem of sudden-show guests. It's the fair thing to do for your guests who have shown respect.

You may not agree with my terse solution. I come by it after years of experience and frustration with exploding guest counts. Do what feels right to you.

# *Table # 0*

## Table for those who didn't return an RSVP but showed up anyway!

This table does not exist because you didn't RSVP.

This table has no tablecloth because you didn't RSVP.

This table has no chairs, chair covers or sashes because you didn't RSVP.

This table has no plates because you didn't RSVP.

This table has no wine or water glasses because you didn't RSVP.

This table has no silverware because you didn't RSVP.

This table has no food because you didn't RSVP.

This table has no pitcher of water because you didn't RSVP.

This table has no favors because you didn't RSVP.

This table has no centerpiece because you didn't RSVP.

This table has no napkins because you didn't RSVP.

# 3

~~~~~~~~~~~~~~~~~~

## Chalk Artists

Good signage is necessary to direct guests or even to add a sentiment around your wedding day. Chalk artists can provide a refreshing, customized solution that reflects your theme with color, designs, or styles of hand-lettering. Using a special "chalk ink" that won't smear, applied with a specific tool designed for that purpose, they can create directional signs, seating instructions for ceremony and reception, table numbers, and menus.

If you think you want to do this on your own, practice by creating a project months in advance. Knowing firsthand how much time and money it takes will help you make an informed decision to do it yourself or hire it out. As with many craft projects, it's not as easy as it looks. If you don't have the correct medium, you will find that your labor-intensive handwriting or artwork could become smeared or even vanish. If you have your heart set on chalk signage, evaluate all of your options.

**Alert.** Chalk artists have great respect for other artists' work. If there is something that you really like, they may recommend you buy it from an artist who has created that, rather than working to duplicate someone else's artwork. Chalk art is not traced or stenciled; it is done in personal handwriting. Respect the artist's need for time to take measurements and craft the work you want. Give plenty of notice—six months before the wedding is ideal. Expect to pay a non-refundable retainer fee to reserve your wedding date. Because a chalk artist rents the boards, you pay less than if you have to purchase them on your own. Of course, boards are rented for a specific, limited time and need to be returned promptly. A chalk artist can relieve your stress of investment in boards and supplies. It eliminates one more to-do for you: picking up and returning.

A good chalk artist will offer a questionnaire so you don't even have to meet in person. The chalk artist will want the name of your photographer and some direction for a theme. Tell them what type of signs you will need and whether you also want illustrations.

Your strong vision will help the chalk artist, as will your trust in their artistic license. Adhere to deadlines to avoid a rush fee. Be responsive, and try not to change your mind after the work has begun.

Find a chalk artist by exploring craft stores or boutiques where vendors display their work. Your florist and your Wedding Planner are all good resources for recommendations.

PLANNING STAGE

# 11

## More Than Music

# 1

# Professional DJs— a Peek Behind Their Curtain

As you know, I think a good DJ is the most important vendor at a wedding. Conversely, a bad DJ is the worst vendor at a wedding. People assume it's all fun and games for DJs. Yes, it's their passion; but it's also a lot of hard work. Setting up, and tearing down can take up to three hours. A good DJ puts in hours of work before the wedding in addition to consultations. They may have to travel to attend rehearsals, conduct a venue check, or to meet with other vendors. The DJ needs to see the venue's floor plan and accessibility to electrical outlets. While it should be a given, I've sometimes had to fight a venue for adequate space and location for the DJ's equipment to be near the dance floor so he could read the crowd.

**Sound systems.** Most DJs or Wedding Planners don't fully trust the in-house sound system that a venue offers. Those systems may be good for the spoken word, but sometimes not even that. A venue may forbid a DJ to use the in-house sound system because a previous inexperienced customer destroyed the system. A professional DJ usually prefers to bring their own equipment.

**The hub.** DJs do more than "just play music." They are the hub for cues about what happens next. DJs can keep the whole team of vendors on the same page at all times. They need to know if there's a delay in the kitchen or a mishap that will throw a monkey wrench into the timeline. DJs have the microphone! If an announcement needs to be made, they deliver it! As a Wedding Planner, I never create a timeline unless it syncs up with the DJ and photographer.

**Do your research.** Learn about a DJ through review sites such as Wedding Wire, The Knot, or Yelp, as well as the DJ's website. That prepares you for the questions you want to ask and to know what you might be asked. To do the best job, a DJ wants you to communicate what you want and inform them of any changes in your timeline or your playlist. They need a list of the names of attendants (maid of honor, best man, groomsmen, and bridesmaids), so they can announce them for a grand entrance, a toast, and other activities that they are involved in. Be sure your DJ knows how to pronounce each name—offer a phonetic spelling with accent marks so they don't stumble over names. It doesn't have to be a foreign language to cause confusion. For instance, is Mia pronounced *Mee'-uh* or *Mī'-uh*? Is Millar pronounced Mil-ar' or Mil'-er? I've seen DJs pace the floor trying to memorize the names before a reception. It's not easy!

A good DJ may ask about family dynamics of the bride and of the groom, favorite memories and songs. And, of course, they need to know the guest count, the theme, the vision, and the flow of the wedding and reception. These questions aren't intrusive—rather, they are designed to help make your wedding day a story about your lives and your future by emphasizing what is special to you and your families.

DJs I've spoken with indicate about ten to twenty percent of their bookings come from people who have seen what happened with non-professionals at other people's events. It takes years for a DJ to master the different aspects of the trade, including how to mix music, how to be a good emcee (master of ceremonies), how to run a business, how to develop marketing and sales, how to engage in networking, and participating in industry and trade organizations that support their profession.

Some couples find out the hard way that hiring an inexpensive DJ can increase stress. I've known people who paid a deposit to a DJ and then never heard back, even after repeated attempts to connect. Hire someone who is experienced and trusted, so you don't waste time and money and ramp up your stress level.

**Psychology.** An empty dance floor at a wedding is not a good sign. A good DJ will interact with an audience to entice them to dance. Psychologically, the size of a dance floor matters. If the dance floor is too large, guests might feel like they are entering a fish bowl and be too noticeable. If the dance floor is too small, they might worry about overcrowding and avoid dancing altogether. Ask your DJ or the vendor that rents out the dance floor what size they recommend for your guest count. Some venues have a built-in dance floor. The typical dance floor is twelve feet by twelve feet. Ironically, that is also the size that is recommended in interior design for a comfortable, seated conversation area.

**Science.** If you are afraid that people will leave your reception early, music entices guests to stay longer, and they remember more about the event. Science has shown that music impacts multiple regions of the brain. When patients with Alzheimer's Disease or other forms of dementia hear music, they often break into song, singing the correct lyrics and staying on key after years of vocal silence. Singing and listening to music triggers emotions and helps with memory recall.

**Expertise.** Have you ever been to an event where the music actually felt annoying? Not all venues are created equal when it comes to acoustics and how the music will sound. An experienced DJ will recognize the challenges of a particular venue and can help determine if there is an issue or not.

**Booking.** While it's best to book a DJ six months to a year ahead of the wedding day, it can't hurt to ask a good DJ five or six weeks out from your wedding. Do your best to make it easy for the DJ, whether or not it's a last-minute decision. Appreciate their extra effort and let them know that you do.

**Communication.** Respond quickly and completely to your DJ. Don't leave blanks on the consultation forms or contracts. The absence of data will delay the process. Supply all the email addresses and phone numbers that they ask for, as sometimes they need to make quick decisions and can't do so with insufficient information. DJ's especially need you to avoid last-minute changes.

**Payment.** Pay your DJ promptly. First will be the retainer payment of 50%. If final payment isn't made before the wedding, the DJ does not have to show up. Their service isn't a concrete item that they can hold hostage, like a car in a repair shop, until you pay the bill. And remember, you don't pay them a deposit; you pay a retainer fee. The retainer assures they will decline all other business for your reserved date. If you skip out on a payment, they have no obligation to show up at your wedding.

**Professionalism.** Know whether the DJs you interview own their own business or work for someone else, or just do this on the side. You will get what you pay for. Ask about the quality of a DJ's equipment and if they have good backup equipment. You may get different services at different price points, so do your research. You don't want to hire an impostor who looks and sounds like a DJ, but can't back that up on the day of the wedding. How much skin do they have in the game?

**Etiquette and common sense.** DJs don't appreciate rude or intimidating behavior any more than anyone else. A wedding reception isn't like a club or a Karaoke bar. Your DJ has to think in three-minute increments, and that can't happen if he is taunted with interruptions from people other than the bride and groom. A guest might request a song, but what if it evokes unpleasant memories for the couple? Not good. The last thing the happy couple needs is to hear a song that was "their song" from a previous relationship. Oops! Help your guests understand that it's *your* wedding, and all of the music has been specifically chosen by you to create the wedding day of your dreams. A professional DJ (unlike a friend or family member with an iPod) will have access to music that is "kid friendly" and "elder friendly."

**Honesty is the best policy.** It seems like a no-brainer, but be honest with your DJ. Someone who tries to fool a DJ is only fooling themselves. Don't tell a DJ that you are planning a kid's birthday party in order to save the more expensive wedding-event rate. Not only is it disingenuous, but it will likely backfire, as the music selection and attention to detail will be vastly different than you hope. Would you invite people to your wedding under pretext of it being a child's birthday party? Show your DJ the same respect you show your guests.

# 2

◇◇◇◇◇◇◇◇◇◇◇◇◇◇◇◇◇◇◇◇◇◇◇◇◇◇◇◇◇

# The iPod Wedding

A DJ is the glue that connects all the moving parts of a reception. An iPod can't announce that someone left their lights on in the parking lot. It can't keep all the vendors a step ahead of what's next so everyone can be prepared. Unattended iPods don't direct tables to the buffet line or make emergency announcements. The DJ communicates announcements among everyone at the wedding. A DJ informs people and relays messages if changes are made during a reception.

An iPod cannot be the eyes and ears to your wedding and reception, it can't give instructions, and it won't notice when the floor needs to be cleared to make way for a surprise element. It can't manage the flow on the dance floor. And I've seen non-professional DJs forget to choose music for the recessional, so the newly married couple walked in silence back down the aisle. It felt more like a funeral than a wedding.

If you think all you need for a wedding ceremony is to whip out an iPod and play a processional and a recessional, think again.

Consider these points: Has the person programming the iPod researched all of the versions of a song? A shorter version may not be long enough to fill your time and will leave you in awkward silence. An iPod won't make recommendations even better than what you had in mind. An iPod won't read the crowd and know what to queue up to set the tone for different parts of the reception. A DJ will adjust the sound level (based on experience) for the most comfortable decibel level for the crowd and will know the neighborhood, city, and county ordinances governing noise level. An experienced DJ is your best bet.

If you do use an iPod for your music, practice before, during, and after the rehearsal to be sure everything is finely tuned. Confirm that whoever is in charge of the iPod is willing to stay with the iPod for the entire wedding

◇◇◇ 124 ◇◇◇

and reception and that they will stay sober! Will your iPod "manager" be available for you at all times if you need to tell them something? Will they behave with the temperament of DJ/master of ceremonies or nightclub DJ? Will they read the crowd, and do they know what kind of music will fill a dance floor? Whatever you do, create a timeline for the person in charge of the iPod. That will be their new best friend during the reception.

# 3

‹‹‹‹‹‹‹‹‹‹‹‹‹‹‹‹‹‹‹‹‹‹‹‹‹‹‹‹‹‹‹‹‹‹‹

# Live Music

People sometimes don't consider hiring a live band or a combination of instrumental and vocal musicians, if they aren't familiar with what a live band offers as compared to a DJ. For some unknown reason, people resist hiring a vocalist with accompaniment in fear it will be too loud or not appropriate for background music. That fear is basically unfounded in the case of professional vocalists. Some professional musicians can also emcee your event and make announcements between songs or music sets, eliminating the need for a separate emcee. Professional performers will bring their own sound system that can be controlled to match the ambience you want.

**The pros.** Professional musicians invest their lives perfecting their craft, spending tens of thousands of hours practicing, taking lessons, studying, and learning from the best. It is both time consuming and expensive, but they do it because it is their calling and their passion. If a client requests songs that are not in the band's current repertoire, it necessitates editing and arranging sheet music and learning and rehearsing the songs in advance of the event to fulfill their client's wishes. Good professional musicians will do this. It's an art form that takes a lifetime of development to accomplish and to sustain a high-quality performance. Live musicians are often comparable in price to DJs, so don't dismiss the idea. You know what you like and the atmosphere that you want. You have options.

Decide if you like a performer's music and style by visiting their website and listening to their sample recordings. If you like their style but not the sample selection, contact them and see what else is in their repertoire. The Musician's Union in your city or nearby is a good place to find musicians to fit your taste. Here's an online directory of musicians around the country and around the world: https://randyhalberstadt.com/directories/. Music is like food—sometimes it's best to do a "taste" test. If you have an opportunity to hear a performer live, it can be a fun research project.

**Surprise!** Live musicians can create an atmosphere unlike recorded music. A harpist can bring a level of sophistication or elegance to a ceremony or a reception. A high caliber vocalist/harpist duet can give you goosebumps. I was surprised and delighted when I heard Led Zeppelin music coming from a harp. Imagine the laughter of people dancing to rock music from a harp. It's fun and a bit of a head-turner, and your guests won't likely forget it.

**Logistics for going live.** Musicians for outdoor weddings and receptions need shelter and adequate electricity. They will need a venue tour with you or your Wedding Planner to get the lay of the land and plan for unloading and loading. They need to know the terrain, how many stairs to climb, and what type of ground surface they will be dealing with for set-up. And they need to know when they can arrive to set up without interfering with the ceremony.

**Say yes to both!** If you want, you can have both a live performer and a DJ. A harpist or a vocalist can perform pre-ceremony and ceremony music, and the DJ can play for the reception. Consider harp music, an instrumental quartet, or a vocalist during the dinner or for a special dance.

**Payment.** The standard 50% retainer usually applies for musicians as it does with most vendors. They will expect final payment within the month before the wedding, or they have no obligation to show up and perform.

# 12

# The Vendors Who Document Your Day

# 1

◇◇◇◇◇◇◇◇◇◇◇◇◇◇◇◇◇◇◇◇◇◇◇◇◇◇

# Photographers

Professional photographers take extreme pride in their work. Each one has a unique style of capturing moments, and their experience shows. The word *photography* literally means the study of light, and it is both an art and science. Each different photography specialty requires continuing education on updated methods and the latest technology. Wildlife photography, senior portraits, family and newborn photo sessions each require a special set of talents. But do know that the skill set alone DOES NOT make a good wedding photographer. A professional family or real estate photographer is not the perfect solution for wedding pictures. Intentions may be good, but the wedding pictures may not turn out how you expect.

**Equipment.** Wedding photography requires a quality camera, but it doesn't end there. Ink for wedding photography is of a higher grade than for other photo development. You may have noticed a vast difference between photos printed at different stores. And none of them likely compare to a wedding photographer's prints. A good photographer invests in the right equipment and materials to produce the best photos, and may expend a healthy sum on insurance as well. The costs of running a photography business, whether or not it involves a brick-and-mortar studio, are substantial.

**Teamwork and partnerships.** Most photographers often have a second shooter (an additional photographer) for weddings. More than any other wedding professionals, you will see husband and wife duos in the business of wedding photography. A duo's work is often so similar in quality and artistic format that it's hard to tell who took a specific shot. Hard to explain. It's also not uncommon for a husband and wife to be a photographer and videographer team. If you aren't working with a husband-and-wife team, ask if the photographer has a second shooter *of the opposite gender.* This is a practical consideration for photographing the bride and her attendants and the groom and his attendants simultaneously. It makes for fewer uncomfortable surprises in the dressing room. Personally, I wouldn't hire a photographer who hasn't worked as a second shooter for a professional photographer before striking out on their own.

**Preparation time.** A professional photographer spends time prior to the wedding to be sure there are extra batteries, equipment and materials are clean, and backup plans are in place in the case of equipment failure. Photographers have to turn on a dime to get unique shots, and that can mean a quick change of the equipment and materials in a limited span of time.

For each hour of shooting a wedding, a photographer spends on average at least three to four hours editing. During peak wedding season, no need to be on the edge of your seat. It may take longer to get your pictures when you're not the only client in the queue.

Establish a good relationship with your photographer. Know if their style matches what you envision for capturing the moments of your wedding. One way to know this is to have an engagement photo session. Many photographers will include an engagement session at no cost if you hire them for the wedding. Plan on a few hours, perhaps in several locations, for a good photo shoot. And if the photographer doesn't make you comfortable enough to make you smile and laugh, you need to keep looking.

**Photo apps.** There are apps for your phone that enable guests to upload their candid reception pictures to a common place. The features of these applications vary. Ask your photographer which app they recommend. A photographer may advise you to consider the behavioral maturity of your guests. Will you get the shots you want or ones that will disappoint you? And remember that you might not see the pictures until much later, after the guests have posted pictures to social media.

**What your photographer wants you to understand.** Photographers prefer an unplugged wedding, at least during the ceremony. That means all electronic devices are turned off during the ceremony, except for the photographer, videographer, DJ, and the officiant. Whoever is conducting the ceremony can announce the request several minutes before the ceremony as well as right before the processional. Don't start the processional until it looks like all electronic devices have been stowed.

The DJ, officiant, and photographer have to be perfectly synced at that moment. They also need to be in sync during the reception, so they can get good photos of special moments like the first dance, father-and-daughter dance, etc., while everyone is competing for space and blocking each other's shots. At the reception, the DJ can ask the guests to allow the photographer and videographer to get those important first shots of the cake, toasts, and special dances. There will be plenty of pictures taken of guests during the reception. It's good for family and guests to remember that a couple has paid a good amount of money to have high-quality pictures taken for their lasting memories. The photographer's positioning takes precedence. Most photographers will post the photos in an online gallery for guests to view.

Wedding photography can be hazardous when guests jump out of their seats, step into the aisles, and raise their arms to get a shot. Not only do other people's cameras, phones, and tablets interfere with the carefully calculated lighting, but it amplifies the sounds of the clicks of their cameras. Electronic devices can also interfere with the sound from the DJ's perspective.

**Be decisive.** Photographers like it when a couple is clear about what they want photographed. Do you want photos before the wedding rather than afterward? There's the moment of "first glance"—when a couple sees each other before the ceremony so pictures can begin earlier. When the groom has been given orders to stand still and not look back while the bride sneaks up, that's the setup for the first glance. The first glance prior to the ceremony can actually calm your nerves, but no one will force you to have a first glance before the walk down the aisle if you don't want to ruin the moment for the real-time event. And if you worry that a first-glance photo will rob you of reactions during that walk down the aisle, you probably have nothing to fear. It's like there are two magical moments instead of one, and both offer a sense of relief. The love of your life is the first person you want to see. How can you ruin that?

Photographers help you develop a customized shot list. The list determines how much time they need to take all of the pictures you want. The first glance will save you time after the wedding, as you've already posed for the prime shots. Your guests won't have to wait so long to be fed. You won't have to spend extra money on a cocktail hour while all the pictures are being taken. And, having worked up an appetite by now, you can eat sooner than later.

Couples often want to focus on fun or rambunctious shots, but your photographer will recommend you balance the mix with still or portrait shots. Ten, twenty, or thirty years down the road you will appreciate that not every shot is of someone jumping in the air, etc. If there is a current fad for wedding pictures, remember: Fads fade fast. Future generations want to know what their ancestors looked like. In the same way we are entertained and intrigued by our parents' and grandparents' styles and attire, future generations will think you wore ridiculous, outlandish, or nostalgic fashions. Speaking of jumping in the air, florists are dismayed by bouquets that end up in tatters for the ceremony pictures because people have been raucously tossing them in the air. Florists love to see pictures of the flowers being used at the wedding. Save the acrobatic photos for after the ceremony.

As the wedding season approaches, photographers have many clients to serve, and they need couples to respond quickly. You don't help the photographer by saying you don't care or you have no idea what you want. Research the photographer's work and know their style. Identify what you like about their work. Visit their blogs to gain appreciation for what they do. That will create a better relationship for everyone involved.

**Makeup.** Photographers appreciate coordination with a professional makeup artist. I attended a meeting where a photographer and a makeup artist demonstrated how different the outcome is with and without professional makeup. Fun (or not so fun) fact: In photographs, makeup with glitter looks like sweat. Even brides savvy in everyday makeup application can use the touch of a professional. Great photos—because of the professional lighting—require makeup suitable to be filmed on the set of a TV station

**Timing is everything.** Don't expect to get full coverage of your wedding and reception in two hours. Your photographer will develop a package for you based on what you want to capture. Be realistic about the time required. The photographer's work doesn't end when the wedding day is over.

Don't be surprised if a photographer asks if you have a professional Wedding Planner or a day-of coordinator. Working with a planner or coordinator makes their job much easier and lets them rest assured that they won't be taken away from their own responsibilities.

When you love looking at your wedding pictures (especially if you usually don't like pictures of yourself), you will know that your time to find the best photographer for you was a good investment!

# 2

# Videographers

A videographer brings value in so many ways you might not even realize until after your wedding is over. They capture the moments that people will bring up in conversation for weeks, months, and years to come. Videography forever captures the sights and sounds of your wedding that you weren't aware of in the moment. You will laugh, cry, gasp, and cover your mouth, and then chuckle when you watch your video. Years later, you will be touched when you hear the voices and conversations of grandparents and parents. You will be in awe of how much the little kids have grown. I wish you a long and happy marriage, so you can reach the point when you wonder how in the world you thought those bridesmaid dresses were so cute. The video is also great entertainment for future kids when you want them to sit still for a few minutes. A videographer brings comfort in your future—not just as a tool to make kids sit quietly, but also as a stroll for you down memory lane.

**Teamwork.** A professional videographer will work with the other professionals at your wedding, especially your photographer. Before you hire a photographer and a videographer, ask them if they have ever worked as a team. As professionals, they should talk with each other before the wedding about how they will work together to create what both of them know you want. If they aren't willing to do that, consider searching for a different pair.

Videographers and photographers both will want shots of the entire reception area, including the table decorations you invested in, before people are seated. A videographer cannot photoshop out coats, purses, or clutter, so they need to work when the reception area is fresh. Let your guests wait for a few minutes to enter the room, not only for the Videographer and Photographer to take those shots, but for you to bask in the beauty of it all. Your Wedding Planner can help coordinate this.

**Go for the pros.** Friends and family members can shoot videos with their camera, but likely the quality their equipment falls short of what a professional videographer will use. A good videographer is well trained and has invested in secure backup, ensuring your videos won't be lost. They realize the minute details that others don't think about, like choosing background music and purchasing the permission to use it. Many a clip has suddenly disappeared from YouTube because it used music without permission. A professional will know how to distribute the video to different online platforms.

If you wait until the last minute to consult with a videographer, they may do their best to accommodate your wedding date. But show them the courtesy of time. It is preferable to give them six to twelve months' notice. Check out their gallery of wedding videos to see their quality. Some videographers have an additional still video camera set up to compliment the shots they take during the ceremony. Each has an individual style. Find one who resonates with you. Do you want the scene to play like a documentary, like a fairy tale, or something else?

**Help your videographer.** Fully complete all of their forms and questionnaires for the consultation appointment. Refine and complete the planning with phone calls and emails. Details, communication, and prompt responses to their requests are crucial.

**Vendors learn from other vendors.** As I interviewed vendors for this book, I learned something to improve the timelines I create for future receptions. The time for a videographer to shoot the cake cutting, first dances, or toasts often coincides with the time that wait staff are clearing plates. The background clatter makes it harder to hear the voices of those special people. It's helpful to the videographer to schedule the table clearing either before or after the special moments.

# 3

# Photo Booths

Photo booths provide entertainment at a reception and can also take the place of favors. People can take home a fun memory to share with friends and family for a good laugh. Party favors just aren't as much fun!

Photo booths are not a snap. A photo booth is more than simply software on a screen. The product from a booth that uses inferior ink doesn't compare to that from a dye sublimation printer (DSP). DSP photos are similar in quality to passport photos—the colors will not run or be damaged by water.

It takes four to six hours to prepare the graphics and program the photo booth software before an event. A good photo booth will produce a picture immediately and be available for social media links. Other factors in the cost of a photo booth include storage rental for all of the equipment and props plus the cost of insurance.

Check out the age of the photo booth equipment. Booths from the early 2000s offer lower quality because of the advancements in ink and dyes. Older booths may not easily upload to social media platforms. Unless all of the photo booth equipment is of the highest quality, you might be disappointed in how long the pictures last. The industry changes quickly, so do your research.

Photo booth vendors are often an afterthought when there are a few dollars left in a couple's budget. If that's the case with you, be realistic and know that you get what you pay for. As with any other vendor, do your research and know your budget.

A good professional photo booth vendor will have attendants at all times, and it doesn't take long to figure out why. Photo booth vendors put up with bad behavior and assumptions by the guests, like *I thought there would be hats*. If kids will be using the photo booth, hats can be a transmitter of lice. Ick!

Photo booth vendors will appreciate it if you don't consider the booth as a primary source of entertainment for kids. The combination of kids and a photo booth can be a dangerous and expensive. Don't let your guests use the photo booth as a babysitter.

Photo booth props (which can be costly) are meant to stay at the booth and not to be worn elsewhere at the reception. The props are not favors! They are the property of the photo booth company.

I wasn't at all surprised when photo booth vendors told me they appreciated it when their clients have a professional Wedding Planner. The next time I am hired for a wedding with a photo booth, I will be an extra set of eyes to monitor behavior.

# 13

## Making it Legal

**The Officiant.** I've been a wedding officiant and a Wedding Planner for many years, but I didn't want to limit this book to things only from my view. There are common threads among officiants and what they encounter. A common misconception is that officiants are paid to talk for twenty minutes, but unless you're getting married by a justice of the peace at the courthouse, a lot more goes into the ceremony.

A judge charges about the same as an officiant, but the officiant performs a custom ceremony and will attend the rehearsal, as well. Rehearsals can take two to three times as long as the actual wedding ceremony. Getting everyone in the wedding party to the rehearsal is harder than herding rabbits in commuter traffic on Friday evening. You've heard about the invisible rabbit, Harvey? That might be your best man. He may be your friend, but he's nowhere to be seen.

> *Consultations.* Officiants have different styles of consultation, and that can affect the look and feel of a ceremony. Find someone who has experience performing ceremonies, who won't be nervous, and who will make you comfortable and at ease. Look for someone who resonates with your style and your personality and who is open to your ideas. Be sure your officiant knows the laws for waiting periods and other requirements before a wedding can take place legally in your state. Some states require the officiant to be a religious leader in a physical church. The laws apply across the board: to ministers who are ordained online, to ministers affiliated with a physical church, to judges and justices of the peace. In general, for a marriage to be legally recognized, a couple must prove that they are not entering the marriage under duress, and the officiant has to declare or pronounce that they are legally married. Each state differs.
>
> An officiant has the right to decide if they will perform a wedding ceremony; if a couple appears intoxicated, or if it appears that one of the parties might be entering a dangerous marriage, the officiant can just say *no*. An experienced officiant knows what to look for.
>
> Professional officiants will carefully review and complete the paperwork that makes the license valid, and they will see that it is properly filed with county and state authorities. If your officiant

is a friend who was ordained online and doesn't have experience with the paperwork, ask for help. Because I am both an officiant and a Wedding Planner, I can assure a couple that if the minister doesn't show up, they will still be married that day. I always ask for a copy of the ceremony, just in case. I came within ten minutes of having to perform a ceremony at one wedding because the minister got terribly lost. For a small wedding that required no setup, I have acted as both officiant and day-of coordinator. If I'm going to officiate, I'd prefer to not be sweaty from setting up a venue, so I always hope the minister shows up!

Officiants want to know their clients on a level different from other vendors. Officiants deal with the serious part of the wedding—the part that will count the most at the end of the day. It's easy to feel concerned about the party, but the wedding ceremony is a celebration acknowledging that you have found each other and want to spend the rest of your lives together.

Some couples have a courthouse ceremony and then, months or years later, have a "real wedding." This is common for people with military deployments who opt for a quick civil ceremony then a "second" wedding upon returning home. Legally, their marriage is recognized as the date of the original ceremony. It's critical to let your officiant know if this is the case, and to tell them who, if anyone, in the family or the bridal party knows about it. People expect to see pictures of the couple signing a document. That document is usually the certificate, as opposed to a license, and that can be re-created, since it's not the legal document. I have customized some certificates for that very occasion!

I've seen a couple who pretended that they had a marriage license, but when it came time to sign on the dotted line, the officiant discovered there was no license. In this scenario, it's the couple's responsibility to make their marriage legal at a courthouse or have an officiant come to their home to perform a small ceremony with witnesses once they have their license. Their legal marriage date is the day of the licensed ceremony, not the party that took place beforehand.

An officiant might ask you about your lives together, how you met, what your hobbies are, what you do for a living, what you liked or disliked about other weddings, and what you dream for your future. All of that shapes a meaningful ceremony. Once your officiant has drafted the ceremony, you should review and approve it.

*Logistics.* An officiant wants to know the theme, physical layout, acoustics, and any other details to determine if there might be trouble spots to take care of before they become a problem. As with any other vendors, advise the officiant immediately if there is a change of venue. The officiant will want to know how you want them to dress. A professional DJ can remove the technical unknowns for an officiant's performance. Logistical problems might be resolved by creating a custom ceremony. One couple who wanted an outdoor wedding wanted programs to be set on each chair. To keep them from blowing away in the wind, they created a rock ceremony that became a very sentimental part of the wedding. Family members in another state collected rocks from a lakeshore where the bride's family had a cabin for generations. Each guest put a rock into the box with a silent good wish for the couple. The couple placed the first stones in the box as the "foundation." One of our couples painted *Faith, Hope,* and *Love* on three separate rocks and placed them at the bottom as their foundation.

*Ceremonies.* Get acquainted with various types of ceremonies. There's a rock ceremony, sand ceremony, jumping-the-broom ceremony, unity candle ceremony, rose ceremony, and handfasting ceremony. There's even a wine box ceremony, where the couple writes love letters to each other and puts them with a bottle of wine in a box to open and celebrate on their first anniversary. Some people tweak this and open the box when they have their first argument after they are married.

An officiant can craft into the ceremony a reminder for friends and family to support the couple, to promote success in their marriage, and not to be a hindrance. Unless there is suspected abuse (in which case, professional counseling is recommended), families need to respect the space that every couple needs to have a happy marriage. This acts as a reminder to guests of the sanctity of their own relationships, as well.

Some people adopt traditions from other cultures for their wedding ceremonies. One couple we worked with wanted Jewish elements in their wedding, including the chuppah (a ceremony canopy), the breaking of the glass, and seating the bride's family on the right. My husband and I thought for certain that was part of the heritage for one of them. We felt compelled to research Jewish weddings and thoroughly enjoyed what we learned. At the rehearsal, it dawned on us that we assumed incorrectly when someone asked when they should say, "Mazel Tov." They wondered if it would offend anyone at the wedding who might be Jewish. Nonetheless, our research on Jewish weddings was useful! Each culture has so much to treasure. It's a privilege to live in one of the most culturally diverse areas in the country—and to know that love is love and tears of joy are universal.

*What's in a name?* I have yet to have an officiating consultation where a fiancée or a fiancé doesn't say, "I never even thought about that!" We don't know what we don't know. Among other things, couples often haven't considered who will or will not take the other's last name. This surprises me—it's kind of a big deal! So far, no fights have broken out when I've brought it up. It usually comes up when we discuss how they want to be introduced after they are pronounced husband and wife, husband and husband, or wife and wife. Sometimes they will be introduced in a traditional way, even though they will be living their future lives together with a different name combination. Often, the name recognition in a career field plays into the decision to take another's name or not. I respect whatever they want.

*Rehearsals.* Not all officiants attend rehearsals. If an officiant is booked for more than one wedding in a day, or the wedding takes place early in the day, plan the rehearsal to be a night or two before the wedding. It may seem logical that if your wedding is on a Saturday, your rehearsal will be on Friday. But during a busy wedding season, there's a good chance that won't work. Typically, venues allow rehearsals on Thursday evenings, but even then you may have to share that evening with another couple for their rehearsal.

No two officiants conduct a rehearsal in the same way. I like to start with everyone at the ceremony area, so they can each figure out where they will be standing, how far apart they need to be, and what angle they will face in order for the couple to be visible during the ceremony.

*The cutest!* The ring bearer and the flower girl (sometimes of the canine variety) steal the show because they are cute—and unpredictable. I recommend that any children in these roles be at least three years old and optimally a little older. It's too much to expect any sense of order or discipline for younger children. Expect them to be imperfect—that is part of their perfection. This applies to both kids and animals (I won't play favorites, lest I start an argument). Kneel to eye level for little kids to tell them what to do. Be a kindergarten teacher; speak in terms they understand. Let them watch part of a wedding movie days or weeks ahead. I've found that the ring bearer will exhibit greater responsibility and sense of pride if he names the pillow he will carry. It's not a bad idea in some cases for the best man and the maid of honor to hold the rings, though I have to say that sometimes the ring bearer child is more responsible than the nervous adults. Regardless of how stunning the entire wedding party looks, the little flower and ring duo (kids or pets) is the cutest act.

*Payment.* An officiant may ask for a 50% retainer to reserve your date, with final payment due at the rehearsal. An option is to put your Wedding Planner in charge of distributing final payments and tips at the wedding. That way you don't have to think about it. You have enough on your mind!

PLANNING STAGE

# 14

## Hair Stylists and Makeup Artists

**The preview.** A team that includes a hair stylist and a makeup artist is the jackpot! Especially for a bride, a good makeup artist will not just show up on the wedding day to apply makeup without having done a "preview." A hair stylist doesn't want to experiment with your hair for the first time on your wedding day. There's no time for that! Your stylist will want to know your style and show you options to accommodate that style. They need to know your type of hair, how it responds, whether it can be styled to match a picture that you like. A preview is a trial run that accomplishes many things.

Schedule your preview appointment several months in advance, depending upon the time of year. Set a date at least two weeks or more before the wedding. The most important benefit of a preview is to know if you will have a reaction to the makeup. If you do, you don't want that reaction too close to the wedding day. Be sure your hair is close enough to the length it will be for your wedding, so you can experiment with the styles that you like. Give your stylist some creative license to build on your original idea. Allow plenty of time—schedule a few hours for your previews.

Don't expect a preview for the entire wedding party. Find out how the makeup artist prefers to work. Know if wedding attendants will pay for their own makeup or if you want to pay for it in appreciation for their participation. No two hair stylists or makeup artists are alike. Find the perfect pair for you.

**The veil and the dress.** The makeup artist will apply makeup to your neck and shoulders in addition to your face, so bring your veil and a picture of your wedding dress to the preview. They're the pros, but they will listen to your desires. Let them surprise you. They have done this many times.

Consider tattoos. At the makeup preview especially, let them know about any tattoos you want covered or uncovered.

**Professional makeup.** *Is it okay to use my own makeup?* That's a fair question.

You're going to be in the spotlight, and you want to look your best for your wedding. Camera and lights from any photographer or videographer strongly affect what is needed for makeup. Don't worry! Hair and makeup professionals will be able to accommodate you and give you a very natural look if that is what you want. A professional makeup artist will match your skin tone perfectly with the correct foundation. The camera demands more makeup than usual, as if you were going on stage or TV. It may look over-done in the mirror, but you'll look great in the photos!

Makeup artists have been trained to create the look you want. They know the different elements of makeup and design to accentuate the positive and minimize what makes you self-conscious. They know what types of makeup might be incompatible with the photographer's lighting. Makeup with glitter can be a photo editing nightmare, because in the pictures it looks like sweat. Everyday makeup has a completely different look in a professional photo-graph. I've seen photographs of a bride using her regular makeup, and the photos made it look like she had been beaten up. You will drastically reduce the photographer's editing time when you hire a professional makeup artist, and that means you get the wedding pictures back more quickly.

A good makeup artist will apply sufficient makeup and you won't look like a clown. You will look beautiful! If you're not used to wearing false eyelashes, learn about the different types available. Your makeup artist will help you decide what is best for you.

Makeup artists provide similar services, but check out the extras that set them apart before you make your choice. Extras may be complimentary or for a fee. Extras might be something like making custom foundation just for your face; services for both mothers; accompanying you for all of the photos before the wedding and before the reception. Some will do all of the above. They love what they do and like to stand out from each other, but don't assume that they will provide the extras. If a specific issue is stressing you out, see if you can find someone who can alleviate that. Be aware of the little things that they offer.

Help the hair and makeup artists by not making them wait for the next in line. The bride is usually the last in line so she will be as fresh as possible for the wedding. Ask your attendants to wear a button-down shirt for this preparation, so that their makeup won't be smudged and their hair will stay beautiful after the entire process is complete. Another idea for a thank-you gift for the bridesmaids is a beautiful bathrobe for easy transition from makeup to wedding attire.

Some vendors don't do both hair and makeup, but each professional should have a team and/or should be efficient and in communication with each other so that everyone is done on time without delaying other vendors (primarily, the photographer). Having the right tools and skills of the trade, as with any profession, is the secret to success.

**Late starts.** Hair and makeup are the most common reasons why weddings run late. I'm sure you've experienced that in everyday life. Bringing your hair stylist and makeup artist onsite at the venue or your hotel will save you time and loads of stress over going to a salon on your wedding day. For this to work, your attendants should be in the room with you, so they will be present when the artists are ready for them. You don't need to be herding rabbits. Provide some light snacks such as fruit and cheese and non-alcoholic beverages, so they don't have to go searching to fill the void. They shouldn't be setting up the reception area or taking care of other tasks. Delegate!

**Vendor coordination.** Make sure that everyone is ready and waiting for pictures. Hair and makeup should be done earlier in the day rather than later. Schedule it relative to the wedding start time or the time for pre-wedding photos. You need to know if you even want a photographer for the getting-ready pictures. That could add hours and dollars that aren't included in your basic photography package. People usually feel very strongly one way or the other. The choice is yours. This may be a suitable event for a friend who is already in the room to take candid shots to exchange later. The photography will occupy your bridesmaids while you are trying to keep them trapped in the room!

**Tipping.** Find out the standard in your area for tipping these professionals, and don't skimp!

# 15

## Design and Decor

# 1

# Floral Designers

**Florist or floral designer?** Your neighborhood florist is different from a floral designer. Florists often duplicate designs from the books or websites of FTD or other national delivery services. It is costly for them, because they pay for the privilege to use the designs and they get a very small percentage back or often lose money on those transactions. If you walk into a shop for a quick order, they will likely create something from the cooler of flowers left over from projects. Most can do floral design work and are happy to do so. But ask specifically if they do weddings and look at pictures of their original work.

A floral designer is more suited for wedding flowers than a florist. Floral designers go deep into your story to create designs that reflect you. They don't choose from an inventory in a cooler. They purchase per event to accommodate your needs. They make several trips to the warehouses throughout the week to guarantee that the flowers' bloom cycle is perfect for your wedding day. Different flowers look better at different stages, depending upon the design. Your floral designer will know the perfect timing for a flower to look its best on the day of the wedding.

Working with floral designers is different from working with other vendors. If you ask for a specific type of flower, it can drastically increase the price of your order. Let your floral designer know your color palette, and you will be in a better financial position to allow the floral designer freedom with creative license, knowledge, and experience to create the look you want. It's better to give them a price range rather than giving them a set budget. Pinterest will display wonderful ideas, but whoever markets through social media shows only their best work, which might not fit your budget.

**Flowers cost how much?** The cost of flowers varies depending on the time of year. February is probably the most expensive month for roses, because six months prior to Valentine's Day, growers have to dig up another perfectly good crop so they can grow roses to be just right for that *one day*. It requires hiring extra help to clear the beds, plant, tend, harvest, and transport the roses to various parts of the world. On arrival in another country, they are shipped to distribution centers and warehouses, then delivered to or picked up by the floral shops or studios. The shops store the roses in a cooler before they strip them of their leaves and thorns, trim them, and put them into an arrangement. A lot of hands are required to pull this together! The scenario is similar with Easter Lilies in April—good to know if you're planning a wedding for late March or April.

Additional costs include equipment, supplies, the best tools of the trade, the rental space, employees, delivery equipment, vans, and insurance. Floral coolers are not refrigerators. They are designed to create a fine balance of temperature and humidity.

**It takes a village.** Flowers don't arrange themselves. It takes the skilled hands and eyes of professionals to make a stunning arrangement. With intentional placement, your guests will admire the arrangements for hours. The flowers will become part of their visual memories.

It's hard to imagine a wedding without flowers. Floral designers are professionals, not hobbyists, and they operate as a business. Their work and their artistry put food on their table, like any other job.

Florists and floral designers purchase in bulk. They can't buy just one of a specific flower for your arrangements to display or carry. Knowing the cost of flowers in bulk, it's amazing florists stay in business—until you see the magical difference in what a floral designer can create compared to do-it-yourself buying and assembling. It's a science and an art. Just as shading makes other forms of art come to life, foliage adds depth and texture to a bouquet. Foliage can cost as much or more than the flowers. A bunch of flowers from a grocery store stand shoved into a vase at home looks sparse and bleak compared to the volume, depth, and dimension of a professional floral design.

Important tidbit that bears repeating: Flowers may contain chemicals or toxins; do NOT put flowers on or near a wedding cake before you check to see if they are poisonous.

**The truth—the whole truth—so helps your florist.** Using fewer table decorations and bouquets won't necessarily save you money. Your centerpieces aren't priced per stem. One fewer centerpiece won't likely reduce the floral bill. If your package includes more arrangements than you need, dress up the guest book table, a dressing room, or buffet table. Leftover flowers can be incorporated to create different floral elements. Ask your floral designer lots of questions, and also give honest answers to their questions for you.

Your floral designer will want to know:

- Your timeline
- Where you want the arrangements displayed
- How many stair steps are at the venue
- If your reception and your ceremony are in different places
- Where the venue requires vendors to unload products and equipment

If you have a Wedding Planner, he or she may know these answers, as well as a detailed timeline, and is the key contact person for all vendors. It's a huge stress reliever for you!

**Delivery, placement, and return.** Some brides do not want to toss the formal bouquet. Ask about making a smaller one from unused flowers from your order. Place the smaller bouquet on the guest book table so it will be easily found when it's time for the toss.

Some items, like vases, centerpiece stands, candle holders, wedding arches, etc., are less expensive to rent than to purchase. It's important to know the timeline for your friend, family member, or Wedding Planner to pick up and return items.

**Fresh or artificial?** Some people think artificial flowers are more eco-friendly than real flowers that will end up in a landfill. Artificial flowers are much better quality than they used to be, and they can be used as home decorations. But eventually artificial flowers end up in the landfill, too, and that is much worse for the environment. Artificial flowers are a positive alternative if real flowers trigger allergies.

**Where do all the flowers go?** Cut flowers don't last forever. They decompose or dry up quickly. One option is to donate the flowers after the wedding. Ask if your floral designer or Wedding Planner is connected with a charity suitable for donation. Another option is to have your bouquet professionally preserved. And if you're a crafty, DIY type, you can learn to dry flowers to have as keepsakes. Some craft stores offer flower-drying classes, but the floral designer can refer you to an expert if you wish.

**A word of warning!** If you attach an heirloom brooch or a sentimental item on your bouquet, remove it as soon after the ceremony as possible. As the reception goes on, the heirloom may not be top of mind, and if the flowers are thrown out or donated, the brooch goes with them. Ask someone to remind you—your Wedding Planner, day-of coordinator, or maid of honor. And if there will be photos of bouquets being tossed, stage them after the ceremony and family photos and after any sentimental items have been removed from a bouquet.

# 2

# Decorating

Be open-minded and skeptical at the same time when it comes to decorations. A good decorations vendor will make sure that you get the look that you want. Decoration costs, like clothing costs, can surprise you. That pricey outfit that turns out to be reversible becomes two outfits in one. On the flip side, you can spend a lot of money on something and be disappointed. State your vision clearly and let the vendors work their magic. Examine costs and benefits and always ask questions.

It's easy to underestimate the time required for decorating. Your decorating decisions will be dictated by your theme or how your venue looks without decorations. A venue that already states your theme requires less effort and expense. Do-it-yourself projects can result in big-time buyer's remorse. It looks easier on the video than it is in real life. Time is one of the intangible elements that factor into decorating costs.

Consider what will happen to decorations after the wedding. If you didn't rent them, you will have to either store them, sell them, give them away, or throw them out (not an eco-friendly concept). If you get married earlier in the wedding season, you may have more options to give or sell the decorations you made or purchased to another couple. If you get married at the end of the wedding season, you might save by using decorations that other people have used. Just be sure they match your theme.

**Aisles: the dos and don'ts.** Don't assume that you can have an aisle runner. Some venues consider them a tripping hazard. Outdoor runners especially need to be well secured. If you will wear high-heeled shoes, I recommend using heel caps to prevent sinking into the ground or puncturing the runner. You don't want the aisle runner hanging on a heel!

You can secure an aisle runner at the ends or at the outside edges. Here's how:

## Secure the ends.

1. Ask your hardware store to cut two pieces of flat iron (not the hair straightening kind!) to just less than the width of the aisle runner. (You can find aisle runners in the wedding section of a craft store.)

2. To create a weight for each end of the runner, cut enough of the runner to wrap the fabric around the flat iron several times. (The runners are very long, so you will have plenty of fabric.)

3. Secure all edges of the fabric-covered iron using clear packing tape.

4. Wrap the end of the aisle runner several times around the flat iron that you just covered.

5. Repeat with the other flat iron for the other end of the runner.

*See more details about aisles in Planning Stage 17.*

## Secure the outside edges.

*I worked with a bride whose wedding was outdoors
by a lake. Wind and lakes go together, so securing
the runner was crucial. Here's what we did:*

1. Find fabric in the wedding colors and cut it into eleven-inch squares. I recommend using pinking shears. Because this bride was an accomplished pianist, I used fabric with a musical note pattern.

2. Put ½ cup or more of standard wedding decor glass beads in the center of each fabric square.

3. Cinch up each square with a small, wire-stemmed, silk flower.

4. Cover the wire with ribbon and tie it in a bow.

5. Place them three feet apart along the full length of each edge of the aisle runner.

Some venues place restrictions on aisle decorations. They might let you use real rose petals but require that they be picked up immediately after the ceremony. This is especially true if that same area will be the dance floor later. As beautiful as they are, flower pigments can stain the floor or be ground into the carpet.

Check the rules about silk flower petals as well. Silk petals are a dangerous slip hazard. Silk flowers have legs and wings and end up all over the place, and you don't want to risk injury to your guests or yourself.

**Warning!** I don't know what gets into people, but some think that table decorations are up for grabs. I've seen people try to make off with tablecloth weights, centerpiece vases, and even goblets. Glassware is expensive when you have to pay for what goes missing. It may feel tacky to tell people to leave the decor alone, but consider designating someone to keep their eyes peeled for the occasional kleptomaniac. Another option is to place a card with a humorous statement asking the guests to leave the decor alone. Yet another option is to label the items as property of company ABC, or to place a thank-you note: "Thank you to the XYZ Floral Shop for lending us the vases." Making people think is half the battle: common sense plus good conscience invigorated by a friendly alert.

**Unique decor.** People tend to overlook ice sculptures on the premise that they are too expensive. They do look like a million bucks, but they are inexpensive compared to other things. A beautiful ice sculpture will hold people's attention—they won't notice the minimal table decorations. They can even save you time! A professional ice artist will set up and tear down with safety in mind and find a place for the sculpture to melt without causing damage.

If it stays frozen outside, that can be a nuisance. But the material doesn't have to be shipped, laundered, or ironed. It's simply water! The cost is in the artwork. It's a big bang for your buck, because it is unique, it makes a huge impact, it sets your theme, and it can render other decorations unnecessary. Ice is beautiful, especially when it is enhanced with lighting. Use ice sculptures for small decorations or go big with a bar that is an ice luge to dispense alcohol.

I used the ice sculpture pictured previously at a wedding show on a cold February day. As luck would have it, the heat went completely off in the huge community center. The hosts of the show finally rented a portable patio heater, and people huddled around it in a six-foot circle. Two ice-carved engagement rings were designed into the ice sculpture. Several of us actually cheered when one of the rings separated from the bottom of the ice sculpture. That meant the heater was working!

**Arbors and structures.** Have you ever assembled a wedding arch from a typical craft store? If so, you know how flimsy they are and the challenges they pose. They are often too tall to stand up straight or hold any weight. If you remove the bottom section of the "legs" to shorten it, it easily ends up too short. I inherited a good arbor from a wedding, and I have let my clients use it so they didn't have to worry about tipping over a flimsy arch. Your florist might have an arbor they can decorate and deliver. If there's space in your own yard, you can build or buy an arbor to install there later. Some fathers enjoy contributing their handiwork for the wedding by building arches or pedestals or columns. It's a source of pride and joy, and the result can become an heirloom.

**Careers and hobbies.** A reception theme that honors a career is fun and unique. I've seen clever ideas for teachers, like attaching escort cards to small picks and using apples to display them. Nearly any profession can be represented in a practical or amusing way.

One of my clients had a girlfriend who was an avid tennis player. They took a stroll on the beach, and he presented to her a tennis ball as if he had found it, commenting it was probably some dog's lost toy. She took it from him and made to throw it into the water, when he stopped her. He pointed out the slit in the tennis ball and, lo and behold, the engagement ring was inside!

They followed that theme for several elements of their wedding. The wedding colors were yellow and silver. They used yellow tennis balls for table numbers. They glued silver chenille tinsel stems to the bottoms so that the tennis balls wouldn't roll over. They slit the tennis balls and inserted a card with a graphic of a ring sneaking out of the tennis ball. The cards posted the table numbers. I'll let you guess how he brought the wedding band to the ceremony! (If you do something similar, do it safely. Use a vice to squeeze the tennis ball while you carefully make the slit, and keep your fingers out of range of the blade.)

**Stock up!** If your colors happen to coordinate with any holidays such as Christmas, Easter, Hanukkah, Fourth of July, or Halloween, hit those sales like crazy and stock up on everything: paper goods, plastic utensils, table-cloths, lighting, and anything else you can use or adapt for your theme. Red, blue, green, orange, brown, or pastels are yours for the taking at bargain sales. Saving money feels good no matter what your budget is!

**Placement.** The rule of thumb is not to have decorations or table numbers any higher than the height of your arm from the elbow to your fingertips, unless you have a tall and narrow pedestal with a top surface for a flower arrangement. Be sure people can see each other and converse across the table.

**Think outside the box.** Don't let other people squelch your design ideas. Let your ideas flow and see what emerges. Sometimes "oops" can turn into something better than you imagined. Create to your heart's desire. Rather than lament about what was *supposed* to be, give the new outcome a special name. In our house, we call burned food "flambé!"

# 3

<center>~~~~~~~~~~~~~~~</center>

# Rentals &
# Decorating Services

Wedding and event rentals supply everything you need but don't own. They offer everything from tents to shrimp cocktail forks. The rental items satisfy logistical needs as well as put your signature on your wedding. You can choose colors, style, and sense of taste. You can evoke nature, the urban life, or casual country decor—whatever environments you find familiar or comforting. Maybe you can't get married in the forest, but rentals can transform a space with the ambience you want.

Whatever a guest will handle to eat with, wipe their face with, drink from, look down at, look across at, look up at, sit at, sit on, and dance on is available to rent. You can even rent table numbers.

Don't wait too late in the planning process to consider rentals. Rental companies don't have an infinite supply. Yours is not the only wedding on their books, and it's first come, first served. When you choose your caterer, think carefully about what you might need to rent.

If you think you'll pick up all of the rentals yourself, think again. It can take a van or a bus to haul everything to or from a rental company. Even linens take up more space after an event than before—and they don't smell that great, either. Rental companies often will pick up items from a wedding at the venue on Mondays. Happily pay the fee for delivery and pickup.

Check the rental company's website and compare their inventory to what your venue or caterer provide. Remember, *provide* doesn't always mean free, so triple-check items against cost.

# 16

## Keeping It Safe

# 1

# Limousines &
# Transportation Services

I post, blog, and speak about limousine services at least twice a year, usually around the time of homecomings or proms. My concern is for wedding clients as well as anyone who might have children or siblings planning to hire a limo. Why? Limousine services that operate illegally (and there are more than you would think) can lead to disaster. Tragedies occur when a vehicle hasn't been inspected and isn't insured. This is totally preventable!

Lack of knowledge or conscience are the culprits. Someone buys a used limo, "fixes it up" or modifies it to be longer, and thinks they are ready for business. They don't realize that some models of limousines have been banned due to their design or design modifications. Some older limousines, when broadsided, become fire traps. I'm relieved to see or hear of an illegal limo being towed from a prom or homecoming. Students aren't happy when they discover their limousine has disappeared, but it's better to be safe than sorry.

Rogue operators also make it unfair to legitimate operators who obey the laws, care about their passengers' safety, hire responsible drivers, and carry good insurance. In this section I will use the term *limousine* or *limo* to mean any type of transportation for hire: limousines, taxis, party buses, etc.

**A driver does not a chauffeur make.** Limo drivers and their vehicles must pass state requirements and inspections. Factors include background checks for the driver, correct licensing, and maybe a drug test. Ask for documentation showing these conditions have been met.

A limo isn't always a limo. In some states, a limo will have a sticker to show that it has passed inspection. Larger vehicles will also display a Department of Transportation decal. Don't assume that all limos are inspected and insured. People who avoid the legalities do so for a reason!

Be proactive. Be sure the limos that transport you, your friends, and your family are legal and safe. If you don't see seatbelts, ask if they are tucked in behind the seats. You're paying good money and placing trust in a limousine service provider. A bargain isn't always a bargain, nor is a high price a guarantee of safety.

**Read the contract; inspect the vehicle.** No amount of money saved or spent can compensate for injury or death due to a negligent limousine service. You might not know who your driver is until just before your event. Be sure that all of the drivers are held to a high standard. You deserve nothing less! The National Transportation Safety Board keeps track of limousine accidents in every state, and you can find that information online.

Ask what types of additional services the limo company offers. If navigation into or out of a venue is problematic, consider hiring a limo to transport guests from a designated park-and-ride lot or other pre-arranged lot to and from the wedding. This is especially convenient when the wedding is in someone's backyard. For guests who have had too much to drink, take their keys and call them a taxi.

Limousines are fun. They make us feel like celebrities and should ensure our safety. The atmosphere and the amenities make it memorable. Limousine companies can also provide valet services and lend a formal atmosphere to any event. Compare companies and find out what additional services they offer. Some even offer services inside the venue, such as a coat-check service.

Don't wait until the last minute to hire a limousine service—all the good drivers will be reserved first. If there's no limousine operator near you, the nearest town may have a reputable transportation vendor.

**Limousine fares.** Ask how the limo companies calculate their fees. Do they charge by the hours or minutes of passenger time, or is there a flat fee for the entire time and distance? Does the fee include driving back to their home base when the evening is done? Ask what is included in the price and what packages they offer. Don't be conservative in the estimate of what you need. Tell them how many people will be in the vehicle.

Be safe, and have fun!

# 2

✧✧✧✧✧✧✧✧✧✧✧✧✧✧✧✧✧✧✧✧✧✧✧

# Keep Everyone's
# Belongings & Gifts Safe

**Gifts and cards.** People like the idea of placing gifts near the entrance to the room. Unless you are at a secured site where no one other than invited guests will enter, please don't do that. Choose a place farther into the venue, even if someone needs to carry the gifts to that location. Even that doesn't guarantee that your gifts will be 100% theft proof if the venue is accessible to the public. Some venues offer a room that can be locked or have an attendant to keep the gifts out of sight. If you have no other options, place the gifts under a table with a floor-length tablecloth, and place the table against a wall or in a corner.

We don't like to think people would steal wedding gifts. But a wedding venue can be a risky place if anyone on the street can see that a wedding is taking place, especially at a public place like a hotel or church. Wedding attendees often don't know each other. It's easy to assume a "stranger" is a friend or relative of the "other side." Someone who dresses to blend in can easily enter and take off with the card box or gifts. Put someone in charge of the gift table to receive gifts as people enter. Have them make sure the gift is tagged with the name of the giver. You may want two attendants, one to receive and the other to run the gifts to the designated gift area.

**Other items.** Coat-check companies will accept and guard your guest's belongings as well as gifts. The cost of their service is a good investment. Not only are gifts subject to theft, but so are the contents of your guests' purses and wallets. Coat-check services run a tight ship to prevent the wrong person from claiming any item.

If a coat-check service isn't in your budget, ask someone you trust who is willing to help. Someone who is uncomfortable mingling with people or who feels shy might appreciate the role and take it seriously. Get some hangers and identification tags ready!

**Gift registries.** While a gift registry eliminates the possibility of theft at a wedding, it ups the chance that something might be stolen from your porch. Ask a trusted neighbor or apartment manager to be on the lookout for deliveries and take care of your gifts until you get home. Some registries offer the option of picking up the gifts at a designated location.

Some registries are available with mortgage companies to open an interest-bearing account for family and friends to contribute to a down payment for a home. The deposits are tracked by HUD (Housing and Urban Development) making the gifting process easy for when a home is purchased. Couples can select from participating lenders where they want to establish the account or whomever their realtor recommends that participates.

# 3

## Rules for Guests

**Behavior.** One bad apple can spoil the bunch. Rules for guest behavior should be common sense, right? Yeah, right. Don't underestimate the potential for disruptive behavior. Go with your gut when you make your guest list. If you think someone might fall into the troublemaker category, talk with them beforehand or don't invite them. It's your right.

I've known vendors who were subjected to unprovoked physical attacks and harassment. Their options are to either quit their profession do what they can to adjust for it: raise their rates and make more demands of their clients. These occurrences become what we call "contract changers." Photographers are particularly vulnerable, but they aren't the only ones who have been physically assaulted. When award-winning vendors that my clients hired were attacked, I took a break to seriously consider whether it was worth it to plan weddings—was I paid enough to watch the door for a drunk or irate guest returning with a gun?

It's a shame that guests are increasingly the biggest problem for wedding vendors. Vendors simply want to do the professional jobs they are hired to do. Do your best to protect their safety and their environment.

### Things we want our guests to know:

1.  Please remember that this is not your day, even though we have planned for months for you to enjoy this day.

2.  Please don't draw attention to detract from our wedding. Keep your conversation polite, even if you don't like someone.

3.  Avoid being self-absorbed. It makes everyone feel uncomfortable.

4.  Bad behavior results in unwanted consequences for you and for us.

5.  Please RSVP on time.

6. If you haven't responded by the requested date, please call me as soon as you remember that you haven't sent your RSVP. Let me know at least two to three weeks before the wedding.

7. If you are suddenly unable to attend the wedding, please call to tell me. Whatever your reason, we don't want the added stress of worrying that you got into a car accident.

8. Realize that every guest who doesn't show up after returning an RSVP adds costs to the wedding for food, chairs, linens, cutlery, glassware, and much more.

9. If you don't RSVP but show up anyway, or if you bring a guest you didn't include on the RSVP, you may not have a seat for dinner.

10. Please don't jump into the aisle or in any other way endanger the photographer to take your own photo. We have paid for professional photos that we won't have another chance to capture.

11. Please don't get drunk and misbehave. Treat our vendors and guests with respect.

12. If you plan to drink, please designate a non-drinker to drive you home.

13. If we have invited your children, be responsible for them. Don't leave them unsupervised. We don't want them to be hurt or to hurt others.

**Brass tacks reminders for guests:**

*Arrive on time.* Don't be the person who holds up the entire event by arriving twenty to thirty minutes late. Allow extra time for travel and safe driving on your way to the wedding.

*Common courtesy.* Value your friendship with the bride and groom. Keep past sketchy history out of the picture. Be friendly in your toasting and in conversations with other guests. When you are drunk or argumentative, you darken the memories for the couple and risk ending your friendship. Remember that if you drink, drive, and cause damage, injury, or death, it can come back as a judgment against the newly married couple, resulting in loss of a home, or worse, loss of respect. If you drink, don't drive.

*Respect the photographer.* Don't interfere with the photographer by stepping in front of their shots. Don't put your arms into the air or into the aisle if it will block the photographer's shot.

Phones or tablet cameras can interfere with the sound system and detract from everyone else's enjoyment of the wedding ceremony. You aren't the only one who wants to see the special event. It's the couple's day, not yours. Let the professional photographer document both the wedding and the reception.

*Respect the DJ.* The couple has already consulted with the DJ for the specific playlist that they want. They did that with their guests in mind. This is a wedding, not a Karaoke bar where you can request whatever song you want.

The DJ needs to keep eyes on the crowd, to keep the dance floor full, to make relevant announcements, to stay on top of any technical problems, and to be available at all times for the wedding couple. Their system of thinking in three-minute intervals leaves no leeway for belligerent remarks from guests and "special requests."

*Respect the venue.* Whether the event is at someone's home or a professional venue, the property does not belong to you. Respect it. Refrain from doing anything that you wouldn't approve of someone doing at your own home. Don't pick the flowers, move the furniture, climb statues or stand on top of sculptures, open unlocked doors, break things (or if you do, report it), park outside of designated areas, or voice your opinion on something that is none of your business. Leave it the way you found it or better.

Don't make requests for activities that have not been approved by the married couple in advance. If the couple doesn't want to throw a bouquet or garter or participate in a dance that requires them to be tossed into the air, don't make it an issue and don't push it.

*Mind your children.* Children will be children. If only adults would be adults, the children wouldn't be a problem. A wedding is not a free playday. Instead of assuming someone else will watch them, use this perfect time to teach your children about special-occasion behavior. If your child is loud or fussy during a ceremony, take them away from the area so everyone else can enjoy the ceremony. If you sit at the end of a row, it's easier to escape with a crying child. Considering the potential amount of damage a child can do at a formal event, it's worth hiring a babysitter—for your sake and for theirs. If that isn't possible, ask if the couple has made plans for onsite daycare, or pre-arrange for your children's daycare at a trusted facility nearby.

*Mind and respect your pets.* The only reason to bring a dog to a wedding is if it is part of the ceremony. A dog that has a chance to be around food at a reception is a recipe for disaster. It's also not fair to bring your dog and then leave it in a car. Moderate to high temperatures threaten the life of your pet trapped in a vehicle. Does your pet have separation anxiety? Dogs do what they were born to do: bark and run. If your dog is part of the ceremony, consider hiring a dog-sitter to deliver the dog at the right time and take the dog home when ceremonies and pictures are complete. Be sure the dog is familiar with the sitter well in advance of the wedding.

*No outside food or drink allowed.* Don't bring your own food or alcohol to the wedding (except perhaps baby food). Venues and caterers do not allow outside food. If someone gets food poisoning, the venue and the caterer does not want to be blamed. The couple, the caterer, and the bartending company have calculated how much food and alcohol will accommodate the number of people attending. If a bartender discerns that you have had too much to drink, you will be cut off, regardless of where or when you consumed the alcohol.

*Honor the seating chart.* Seating charts are designed to ensure that everyone has a seat and that people who want to be together aren't split up. If you want to mingle with other friends, do it after the dinner. It's rude to displace someone who has an assigned seat, and there's even a good possibility that some people are seated apart for a reason. Seating arrangements are up to the couple, and it's no small task, especially when people don't respond until the last minute. Don't expect a seat if you didn't RSVP.

*Keep track of your belongings.* A wedding is a place where total strangers gather to celebrate the same event. After an event, shoes, coats, purses, and other items are left, and there's no way to tell who the rightful owner is. Keep track of your stuff, so you have nothing to worry about.

**The perfect guests.** You perfect guests are so appreciated! You are the ones who act appropriately, who volunteer to assist in clean-up after the wedding, who listen to direction rather than take over, who don't start fights or shoot threatening looks across the room, who don't over-indulge in alcohol. Your pleasant disposition makes for a pleasant experience by others. You thank the newlyweds and their families for a wonderful time.

**Note from a Wedding Planner:** We enjoy meeting and serving all of our clients' treasured friends and family. Please let us know if you have concerns. We are there to help you, explain a situation, or voice your concerns where appropriate. We love to chat and exchange smiles if you are feeling a little lonely.

PLANNING STAGE

# 17

## Putting It All Together

# 1

# Prevent a Late Wedding

Following on the list in Planning Stage 16 about what you wish you could tell your guests, face the fact that weddings sometimes start late. As a Wedding Planner, I like to be ready to go fifteen to thirty minutes before a wedding. That doesn't mean there won't be a blip on the screen. Murphy's Law doesn't take time off just because it is a wedding day. But there are things to avoid or prepare for that will help the event start on time. Build in some 10–15 minute cushions of time into your timeline to make up for the blips. You'll feel much more relaxed for doing that. Here are some common reasons why weddings run late, when it doesn't necessarily have to be the case.

**Hair and makeup.** The most common delay is due to hair and makeup. It's not because the hair stylists and makeup artists aren't doing their jobs. More likely, members of the bridal party aren't waiting where they are supposed to be. The hide-and-go-seek game has officially begun! Sometimes it's the bride who wanders around. She thinks she has plenty of time, since she will be the last one to get hair and makeup done. She is easily lured away to make sure everything is right with the reception space, and it's all downhill from there. She needs to stay in her designated place!

Where is the bride? Where is the flower girl? The vendors do not personally know the people in the wedding party, so if Katelyn the fifth bridesmaid is missing, they don't know who to look for. Even if a vendor met the whole team at a rehearsal, they might not recognize them on the wedding day.

Another time stealer is the person (Mom? Sister?) who decides at the last minute that they should have their hair and makeup done, too. A vendor might be forgiving and accommodate that—sometimes they even plan on it. If it wasn't in the plan, someone will have to pay for it on the spot. Going overtime for your wedding will cause the stylist to be late to their *next* appointment. It's not uncommon for hair stylists and makeup artists to book more than one wedding in a day.

**One last smoke.** This tends to happen just before a ceremony or just before pictures are to be taken. Smokers apparently like company, but for some reason they don't all smoke at the same time. It can be a circus of two out to smoke, two in. Two more out to smoke, two more in. I've been known to say in frustration, "Stay where you are!"

**Flight delays.** People aren't always free to take extra time off to fly to a wedding. They won't make the rehearsal or they may be late to the wedding. Unexpected flight delays can make people late. These delays are more common on holiday weekends. Holidays aren't always friendly to weddings.

**One too many parties.** I've seen how people look on a wedding day after drinking too much the night before or even drinking earlier on the wedding day. It's not pretty. As part of a rehearsal, I give a stern warning that it's not cool to booze it up after the rehearsal and then hurl all over people at the wedding. Post-rehearsal activity is a main contributor to people passing out at weddings. Enjoy that kind of partying at the bachelor and bachelorette parties, not the night before a wedding.

**Underestimating setup time.** When you see the perfect "gotta-have-that" idea for a wedding, it's hard not to run to the craft store or go on an online shopping spree. By all means, create your wedding from vision to reality. Make it something you want to stare at forever! That's easy for some. For others, it seems to require a zillion elements. Neither way is wrong. Just know that you might have only one or two hours to set up all those accumulated ideas. I hate to break it to you, but friends aren't as reliable as you would hope on your wedding day. Don't fault them. They're having the adrenaline rush, too. Or they feel overwhelmed by the crowd of people and so many details. Many a creation never sees the event because the couple underestimates the amount of time and how much help it will take.

**Skimping on rental time.** When you see the cost of renting a venue for an additional hour or more, it's tempting to say, "We won't need that much time." That might be your wallet speaking rather than Old Man Time. You will thank yourself again and again for adding cushions of time to your rental agreement. The details, personalities, and stage-fright jitters are overwhelming when everything needs to come together in a matter of minutes or hours. Some venues have an exorbitant fee for running over your rental time, even by a matter of minutes. Those are the minutes when someone is trying to find their lost purse or coat or baby's pacifier. Give yourself ample time, so you don't feel rushed.

**No direction.** One of my biggest pet peeves with wedding venues is the lack of signage. Directional signs are needed outside as well as inside the venue. People don't automatically know where they need to be, especially in an unfamiliar location. Good signage will save time and confusion.

**Road construction.** "Sorry! We got caught in traffic!" You can't control road construction, but you can check construction schedules in your area, for whatever that is worth. Give yourself plenty of time.

Construction delays are bad enough for traveling to a wedding, but what about going home later that evening? That ramp that they said would be closed beginning at 11:00 PM really did close! Delays to the wedding, nightmares after the wedding. GPS devices can help, but sometimes they put you right back to the same place you've been asked to avoid. If you know ahead of time that construction is an issue, print out maps with alternate routes. Your guests will love you.

**Concurrent community events.** Baseball games, festivals, farmer's markets! It's prime time for them, just as it is for weddings. This can affect more than just traffic. As mentioned in Planning Stage 1, unplanned events such as a Little League Championship could be occurring at the other end of the park where your wedding will be.

In this scenario, you deal with traffic, logistics, distraction, and noise. (If you think kids can be noisy, wait until you hear their parents!) An innocent child in the bleachers may find your wedding more interesting than the game, and soon you have a straggler underfoot while you're setting up. I once officiated a wedding on a Sunday, and part of the venue was set up with a TV broadcasting sports. While the couple was dealing with their own family emergency that led to extra people in town for the wedding, the sports team went into triple overtime. Guess how much noise that generated! We managed to get through it by closing one of the flimsy sliding walls, but it was NOT ideal.

**Perfection speed bumps.** Here's to a well-planned, roll-with-the-punches, I'll-laugh-later, grin-and-bear-it wedding. Your guests will never notice if don't straighten that napkin bow one more time. They WILL notice if the wedding is late. Perfection is nearly impossible to achieve, and you can't please everyone, anyway. Best case scenario, everything goes as planned. Sometimes, second best has to do. As the wedding couple, you set the tone. The calmer you are, the less wigged out everyone else will be. Frankly, the guests are more worried about themselves. You'll probably need a wedding survival story in the future to fit in with a group commiserating about their weddings!

# 2

◇◇◇◇◇◇◇◇◇◇◇◇◇◇◇◇◇◇◇◇◇◇◇◇◇◇◇◇◇

# Banquet Styles

The banquet style determines how food will be served to your guests. Differences can be formal vs. informal or more expensive vs. less expensive. You want a style that fits the atmosphere, your venue, and your budget. Budget is affected by the number of people a caterer needs to employ for a specific buffet style. We'll start with the least expensive and go up to the most expensive.

**Reception style.** The term *reception style* means very few banquet tables, or maybe none at all. The tables are smaller cocktail/bistro size, where guests stand with their food and beverage. This style works if you are serving only beverages and hors d'oeuvres. Your caterer and bartender will know what is the best ratio of protein to alcohol to avoid the over-serving of alcohol. I strongly advise you don't serve alcohol without also serving food. For reception style, you will want to provide a wider variety of beverages to lower your alcohol costs. The reception style is a common setup between the ceremony and the reception while the wedding photographs are being taken and the legal papers are being signed. People often expect a full meal at a wedding, so note on your invitations if the only food you will be serving is hors d'oeuvres. The reception style might be called for when the fire department determines the maximum capacity for a room and not how many people can be seated at banquet tables. Room capacity changes according to your banquet style. Ask the venue what their banquet style code is. Fire departments comply with the International Code Council to set the fire code's room capacity.

**Buffet style.** Buffet style means people sit at tables but serve themselves in a buffet line. A two-sided buffet (where people can serve from both sides of the buffet line) will save you serving time and maybe reduce the rental time. It's good for a DJ (or someone) to release tables gradually, so that the food line doesn't bottleneck. (See Planning Stage 6, Section 4 about when, why, and how to feed wedding vendors.) Utensils and napkins can be placed at the tables or picked up by guests in the buffet line. Including them in the buffet line is less expensive. Buffet style is less expensive because it requires fewer or no servers and takes less work to set up the tables. Table setup may entail only glasses and a pitcher of water.

**Family style.** Family style is a compromise between buffet style and a fully plated dinner. Plates are preset on the table. Fewer servers are needed, because all of the food is brought to the table in bowls, platters, or plates to pass around, just like you would for a family dinner. No one goes through a line, except perhaps to get beverages other than the water that is at the table.

**Plated style.** In this formal style, all of the necessary plates are already set on the table along with all of the glasses, stemware, cups for hot beverages, and utensils needed for all of the courses of a meal. The plated style is usually more expensive, because setup can be labor intensive, and more servers are required than for family style. Plated style lends itself to a more accurate order of food and precise serving sizes. It requires a precise guest count and works best when each guest selects their entrée with their RSVP. Plated style requires place cards announcing each guest's menu selection, as the servers need to know which entrée to serve each guest. You can color code or print their entrée choice on the place card.

**Critical factors.** RSVPs and an accurate guest count are critical for every cost of your wedding, but especially for your reception dinner. I'm sure you're not the one who needs to be reminded of that. It's those people that you have invited to your wedding! Retrieving RSVPs that you have mailed out or announced online will likely be one of your most frustrating wedding planning endeavors. People don't realize the impact of this until they are planning their own wedding or other large event. Often people scramble to retrieve RSVPs during the last seven to fourteen days, at which point you have more than enough details and stress to deal with. And you thought weddings were supposed to be fun!

RSVPs are vital for caterer and rental company deadlines. You don't want to be caught without enough food or rentals, nor do you want to be inundated with food and supplies that are not used because someone didn't show up for your wedding. Rental companies don't have an endless supply of any color of tablecloths and other linens. Popular colors are popular colors! Trends are especially apparent in the linens that people choose. The selection is finite for all items, especially on a popular date for a wedding.

# 3

# Assigned Seating

Some clients turn up their nose at the suggestion of assigned seating. "Do we have to?"

It takes careful planning to decide who sits where. I remind clients that their guests will give the same weight to it on the day of their own wedding. Your guests want to know where they can "nest" and what will be their home for several hours. Assigned seating prevents more problems than it creates. It takes some thought, but everyone will appreciate a smoothly run wedding day—especially your caterer and their servers! Here are the pros and cons:

### THE PROS.

Family dynamics are complicated. There will be people attending the wedding who don't see eye to eye, and they aren't always quiet about whatever the issue or family feud may be. Assigned seating reduces potential conflict. Separate tables are like the fences that make good neighbors.

On the flip side, won't it be fun to seat people together who haven't seen each other in ages and will be thrilled to be at the same table! They will value that gift for a long time.

*Lonely in a crowd.* Intentional seating can evoke great conversations and memories. Here's a tip: Put a guest's name on both sides of a place card. The cards can be conversation starters. It's a relief to be reminded of the name of someone whose face is familiar. Conversation is so much easier, especially for people who haven't seen each other in a long time. You can seat guests who don't know anyone else at the wedding with people who share similar interests or knowledge. You can even name the tables to hint at what they have in common: Opera, Fishing, Race Car, Hikers, or Alumni.

*Organize and plan ahead.* Assigned seating requires forethought and precision. Consider your guests and aim to make it enjoyable for them. Don't put someone who is hard of hearing near the DJ's speakers. Protect your cake from mishap by placing it away from kids' tables, tables with heavier drinkers, and high traffic. If your reception room has a stage, put the cake up there and rope off the area.

*Dining space requirements.* A standard 10' X 10' area for each dining table and its chairs allows adequate room for serving staff to navigate. Assigned seating helps the serving staff, because the menu choices and dietary restrictions are printed on the place cards. See Planning Stage 10, Section 2, for how to seat and serve people who didn't RSVP.

### THE CONS.

*Chronic complainers.* No matter where people are seated, assigned or otherwise, someone will complain. You can't please everyone. Don't worry about them.

*The effort.* Assigned seating requires work *before* the wedding, and it is driven by the RSVPs. Your venue will have created a preliminary floor plan. Ask for several copies. There's no right or wrong way to create a seating chart. You know if you're a list person or a visual person, if you like things in 3D, or you love a good ol' spreadsheet. Work on the seating project in a way that you will enjoy it and it makes sense to you.

One way to organize is to use multiple colors of small transparent adhesive tabs. You can assign tables a color, or you might choose to designate a color for different types of guests, such as different families, co-workers, and old friends. You can have a secret "matchmaking table" when you know that certain people want to meet each other or for people who have common interests.

## OTHER CONSIDERATIONS.

*Escort cards.* Display the escort cards for easy pick-up, like they do at trade shows. If you arrange the escort cards in alphabetical order by last name, you can make four relatively equal divisions by sorting into A-E, F-L, M-R, and S-Z. Adjust as necessary if there are large numbers of people with the same last name. This kind of grouping moves people faster, as they aren't all in one long line. In addition to signs, I've used rose petals to mark off the different sections and letters of the alphabet. It's an inexpensive decorating touch to a table that will soon be empty. Use table number holders to show the letter divisions for each grouping, and it doesn't hurt to have an instruction sign on the wall behind or above the table. Some venues have a wall with a bulletin board—you can set the escort card table in front of it and display instructions and alphabetical divisions on the board.

*Table trotting.* Your fabulously organized escort card table will serve no purpose if the table numbers aren't easy to see. When you have assigned seating, you won't be creating a situation where a guest is wandering around and repeatedly asking people if they can have a seat next to them. That it such an awkward feeling.

*Head table seating.* Will there be a head table for you and all of your attendants? Have place cards ready and waiting for them at the head table. Seat the best man and the maid/matron of honor closest to you and your spouse, so they are nearest you when it comes time for their toasts. Consider seating the attendants in the same order that they lined up for your ceremony.

# 4

# Setup

**Visit the venue one more time.** Before setting up, you want to almost know the venue like the back of your hand. It's common for people to return to the venue for one more look, and your vendors will also want see the space if they haven't worked there before. A Wedding Planner can arrange to meet with the vendors individually early in the planning process. That saves you from having to leave work to accommodate each vendor's schedule. Venue visits help determine if all the electrical outlets work, if the space for the DJ is big enough, etc. You can't always do rehearsals at the venue, but ask well in advance for a thirty-minute appointment to introduce the space to your set-up team. If the set-up team can't meet there, take a video that explains your intention for each area.

**The dance floor.** If there is a hard surface on the same level as your reception, all you have to do is set up a perimeter to designate an area for dancing. Or you can rent a dance floor, which makes it abundantly clear. It's okay to put chairs on the dance floor for the ceremony, then clear it for the reception. The dance floor needs to be near your DJ. If a different couple has rented a dance floor the day before your wedding, ask the vendor's permission to leave it there an extra day and see if it merits a reduced price. Other things might also already be onsite: pipe and drape, arbor, etc. Maybe you can split the rental cost. This reduces delivery and pickup costs for the rental company and benefits both you and the other couple.

**Set up the cake table first.** Something people dislike more than cutting a cake is taking responsibility for carrying, moving, or (even worse) setting it up. No one wants to touch the cake until it is on a plate in front of them, ready to eat. Simplify by setting up the cake table first. You'll need two professionals to handle the cake: the pastry chef to move in and set it up and the catering staff to cut the cake.

Remember, don't put the cake out in the open for too long. The cake isn't cut until well into the reception, and you don't want buttercream frosting or creamy filling to spoil from being un-chilled for too long. Ask your pastry chef what temperature is okay for your cake and how many hours you can leave it at room temperature. If necessary, move up the time for cake cutting. Ask ahead of time for a box to preserve any leftover cake and for the top layer to save for your anniversary. Assign someone the task of boxing and refrigerating the cake after the guests have been served.

Allow an unobstructed path on the cake table itself for setting up the cake. The tablecloth, overlay, and a cake stand (if you're are providing the cake stand rather than your pastry chef) can be set up at the very beginning. After the cake is delivered, the decorations can be placed on the cake table along with the cake knife, cake server, two plates and forks, and champagne flutes. Have someone alert your photographer that the cake is ready to be photographed. After the photos, you can place the plates, forks, napkins, etc. on the table for serving the guests.

**Choose your setup team wisely.** If you don't have a Wedding Planner with a team of people to set up your wedding and reception areas, choose a group of friends or family who will work as a team to do the set up. Choose that team wisely. Sometimes, emotionally-mature-beyond-their-years teenage girls are the best. They are eager to help and love to have something to do for the wedding. Choose strong, calm types who will easily understand your vision and carry it out. You don't need someone bossing people around, stirring up tension, and changing your setup mid-stream. You are the captain of your wedding, but you need a crew to keep everything afloat. If you get sucked into the setup, you could be looking at a late wedding. This is your day *not* to work!

**Learning styles.** If your event appeals to the five senses plus one more that I call *quiet,* it will be a success. Keep the senses in mind when choosing a setup team. Offer instructions in a variety of ways so that everyone can be at their best. Put details on paper using both words and pictures. People absorb information through their senses of sight, hearing, touch, or in a quiet environment. If you only give them a list, things will be overlooked. Supplement your table decoration list with a mock-up table, stimulating sight and touch. If possible, select a team of people other than your attendants for setup and decorating. Enlist your teacher friends, if they are willing. Teachers are experts at setting up and organizing space for large numbers. If you don't enlist a team ahead of time, you will be in frantic search of a bridesmaid or flower girl when it's time for hair, makeup, photos, or something else. Divide and conquer. Some vendors prefer to set up their own items, and they are quick and efficient about it. While vendors can be very helpful, it's best to let them concentrate on what they do best and not tax them with things they weren't hired to do.

**Chickens and eggs.** Which comes first? Let's assume that you have rented a venue and you have to set up everything for the wedding and reception. The first step is to prepare your ceremony and reception areas to receive all deliveries and vendor stations.

Place your ceremony chairs and reception tables (set up reception chairs later) first then consider this order to accept deliveries:

1. Decor/Linens
2. DJ
3. Flowers
4. Cake
5. Catering
6. Photo booth

You will save time and confusion if it is obvious where the different deliveries/vendors go. Inform your vendors of the layout, and stick to it. Keep your vendors informed and aim for as few changes as possible. Some vendors will charge for changes made in the last month before a wedding.

**Ceremony area.** The ceremony is the easiest area to set up, even though it might be time-consuming. If possible, repurpose the decorations from the ceremony to be used in the reception area.

In a perfect world, the ceremony has its own designated space that doesn't need to be transformed into the reception area afterward. If the space does need to be converted, sometimes the venue staff will do this for you. Barring either two separate areas or venue staff in charge, your team will need to make the transition, or the *flip*. Flipping the room can take forty-five to sixty minutes, and your guests are getting hungrier by the minute. Plan a space for hors d'oeuvres and beverages to tide them over until the reception. Consider this scenario early on, when you are deciding early on about venues. Does the cost of additional hors d'oeuvres and beverages outweigh the price of a larger venue with two separate spaces or one larger area?

One way to avoid a flip is to combine the wedding and reception. In this scenario, guests are seated at their banquet tables during the wedding ceremony. This is not the most popular choice, but it is a way to make a smaller space workable and save time. Horseshoe-style seating is also an option that combines the ceremony and reception in a single floor plan. For this setup, omit two chairs at each table in the direction of the ceremony, so guests can see the ceremony without twisting around or blocking someone's view. It's like a jar with the lid removed. You don't get as many people per table, but it helps everyone see what is happening. Your venue can provide diagrams or do a special design specific to your guest count. Placing the tables in a staggered formation is another way to increase visibility.

Benefits of horseshoe-style seating:

- You don't need to flip the room.
- You save on food and drinks by eliminating the need for a cocktail hour during the flip.
- You can start the reception sooner.
- It may reduce the venue rental time or it can add a cushion of time for unexpected delays.
- It offers seated guests better visibility of the ceremony and reception.

If you need to set up chairs, tables, or decorations for the altar area and want to accommodate items to personalize your ceremony, consider a small side table to hold a rose, glass of sand, a unity candle, a rock, a wine box, or anything else that will personalize your ceremony or religious activity. Remember to provide adequate space for a DJ, videographer, and photographer to work.

**The aisle.** If you will have an aisle runner or simply scatter rose petals to create an aisle, set up all of the chairs and decorations first. Lay down the aisle runner last, then you can attach a ribbon or garland from the inside chairs of each side to block off the aisle. That directs guests to enter their rows from the outside, without disturbing the aisle runner, which when not secured, can become a trip hazard after people have walked on it. It's somewhat traditional (but seldom done) for a groomsman or ushers to roll out the aisle runner just before the bride walks down the aisle.

Aisle runners from craft or fabric stores aren't always the safest. The better ones are foam-backed. Check out what this company offers: https://originalrunners.com/products.htm. They have everything from plain foam-backed runners to very elegant, custom runners that cost hundreds to thousands of dollars. The benefit of the nicer runners is you can easily calculate the cost per foot. Whether or not they are in your budget, it's fun to look at them simply for the WOW factor! There's a squirrel!

**Guests with disabilities.** Accommodate for guests who rely on a wheelchair by removing a couple of chairs at the end of a row or a corner of the seating area, so they have room to maneuver. If they have a caretaker, take both into account when you design your seating plan. Relay this information to your ushers to help avoid any confusion or unnecessary stress.

**Tables, tables, tables.** Provide your venue coordinator a diagram showing the arrangement you want. They will know how best to configure the space for everything you want to accommodate. If you know how many and what kind of tables you will need, half the event is already planned! Think from beginning to end. Everything and everybody needs a table. DJs often share their space for vendors' personal belongings, but it's nice to include a separate table for vendors.

Help your setup team by letting them decorate the tables before the chairs are placed. Their work will be easier and more efficient. Do, however, label the tables with the table number and the number of guests at each table, so chairs and other items will be correctly placed.

The floor design of many venues depicts perfect 10' X 10' sections ideal for a typical round table and chairs. That design leaves ample space for guests and catering staff to maneuver. Hardwood floors are great if you need to arrange the tables in a straight line. Keep in mind that a staggered design can be more interesting and also make visibility easier for guests. If the floor isn't pre-marked, you can invest in an inexpensive surveyor's wheel to measure any space to help you create and implement your design. It's aesthetically pleasing to have the table legs lined up in the same direction. That makes for uniform tablecloth placement and eliminates the random "high-low" effect.

## OTHER TABLES & SPACES
## TO CONSIDER:

- Guest book
- Gift table (place away from the entrance to avoid theft)
- Ceremony table (for personalized ceremonies/activities during the ceremony)
- Children's activity table (during the reception)
- 2 Vendors' tables (one for temporary staging and one for workspace as they set up)
- DJ
- Cake
- Dessert station or chocolate fountain
- Photo booth
- Coat check, closet, or coat rack
- Caterer tables (prep tables, buffet line, non-alcoholic beverages)
- Bartending tables
- Cocktail/bistro tables for people to set drinks as they mingle
- Optional table for signing the marriage certificate and other paperwork

**Chairs.** If you plan to have chair covers, don't assume they are universally compatible. Sometimes it is less expensive to rent wooden chairs with padded seats than it is to have chair covers. I was day-of coordinator at a venue whose chairs were black, an unacceptable color for the culture of the bride. The chair covers that the bride had reserved did not fit over the black chairs. We went with the padded-chair option instead. Details make the difference.

**Don't overpopulate.** The industry standard of "8-top" means eight people can sit comfortably at the table. Don't try to squeeze ten people around an 8-top. Your guests will feel squeezed and uncomfortable. Physically test out the seating to know what works. Be sure everyone can easily see the head table for the toasts, the dance floor, cake cutting, etc. Chargers add beauty to the place settings, but they take up even more space. Consider everything!

# 5

<svg>⟨⟩⟨⟩⟨⟩⟨⟩⟨⟩⟨⟩⟨⟩⟨⟩⟨⟩⟨⟩⟨⟩⟨⟩⟨⟩⟨⟩</svg>

# The Wedding Night

Now I've got your attention! But don't get excited. I'm referring to what is left to do when the wedding is over and you are well on your way to your honeymoon. What's left behind is not at all romantic. There will be leftovers, half-eaten cake, scattered and unclaimed wine and champagne glasses on every flat surface, wine-soaked linens, and a whole bunch of *what do I do with this?* Plan ahead for what to do with flowers, cake, and food worth saving.

**Flowers.** If you can't take the flowers home, ask your floral designer for a list of places that will accept them. They may even make the delivery for you. For a really big boost to your day, cart them yourself to an assisted living facility. They will beam at seeing a bride!

**Food.** Leftover food is tricky. Health codes outline the parameters for safety, mostly having to do with specific temperature. If the food isn't refrigerated within the required time frame, it can cause illness or worse. The caterers won't automatically make it happen, so check the policies of your venue and caterer. Food that is unsafe needs to be thrown away in order to comply with health codes.

**Lost and found.** People leave behind purses, shoes, coats, pacifiers, sweaters, and even "unmentionables." As a Wedding Planner, I used to hang onto things, hoping someone would claim them, but not anymore. I recommend the bride and groom designate a friend or family member to be in charge of left-behind items.

**Decorations.** Any decorations that are left over and are not rentals to be returned are categorized as lost and found.

**Linens.** The rental vendor should provide a huge canvas bag for return of the soiled linens. If you're the one to return them, be prepared for the odor emanating from your back seat—a heady mixture of spilled wine and food, decaying flowers, and who knows what else!

# CONCLUSION

The wedding planning process is now fully unmasked. Page by page I have revealed some of the psychological, logistical, scientific, and artistic twists that aren't often communicated except in private or client-vendor conversations, if at all. I've busted the myth of some common assumptions, so you don't have to add unnecessary costs to your wedding. I've shown you some options to make your day easier or safer. Most importantly, I've encouraged you to have the wedding that YOU want with your own set of focused priorities, no matter what your budget might be.

This has not been a book of lists. You have been shown the basics of what goes into various parts of your wedding. You've seen options to make your wedding unique or less stressful. You've been given permission not to conform to others' lists that feel restrictive or force you into a box. You've been given the power to feel comfortable working within your own parameters and style.

I hope that the extensive knowledge about what vendors do and why they have to charge what they do empowers you with open eyes. Now you can truly identify your options and know how to assemble a team of great players to plan, prepare, and execute your wedding day. Perhaps you will decide to go with a pro in an area you weren't expecting to hire a professional. Or maybe you've realized that some wedding elements are just not important to you, and that can save you money. Maybe your backbone is stronger, and you can ward off what *They* say and move on when it doesn't feel like you! You may even feel a little smug, suppressing a knowing smile, that you are equipped with psychological armor to deflect arrows of critique and opinion.

Unexpected behavior from your guests won't take you off guard, as you will have a plan to stop or prevent such behavior.

I wish you a lifetime of happiness, even on the rougher days that make the bright days even brighter. When the clouds hide your sun, remember that the sun never stops shining, and it will make you warm again.

Writing this book has felt like planning your wedding. The journey is over, and already I'm feeling the withdrawal. I'm going to miss our little chats from these pages.

I would love to know how this book has helped you. If I can answer any questions or help you as you plan your wedding, please keep in touch through my website www.greatestofdays.com You will want to go there to keep up to date on additional educational tools and events that are being developed to help people plan weddings or other events.

*Love and joy to you, my friend!*

# AUTHOR BIO

Janis Flagg has been in the wedding industry since 2007. At that point in time, she had planned numerous events for people and some of their guests asked if she planned events for a living. From those questions, her passion for creating events that would celebrate, inspire, and comfort transitioned into a business called Greatest of Days.

After several years in the industry, she noticed that the media was fond of throwing the wedding industry under the bus. Seeing an industry she loved being misrepresented and providing nothing to help couples understand the real world of planning a wedding, she was determined to do something about it. She wanted to narrow the knowledge gap between couples and wedding vendors rather than widen it. She also believes that limiting wedding planning to checklists is asking for more stress and not preparing couples for all the nuances of wedding planning and knowing how vendors are unique from each other.

Janis Flagg spent years leading a networking group where she connected wedding venues with wedding vendors. She facilitated 60 meetings at 55 different venues and learned a lot from those who worked in the trenches. She has planned many kinds of events and weddings as well as officiated many weddings.

She truly cares about couples and their families and seeks to help them understand the art, science, logistics, and psychology involved in planning a wedding. *Wedding Planning—Unmasked!* has been written with the same dedication that she has shown her clients.